COMPOSING THE CHEESE PLATE

RECIPES, PAIRINGS & PLATINGS
FOR THE INVENTIVE CHEESE COURSE

BRIAN KEYSER & LEIGH FRIEND

RUNNING PRESS
PHILADELPHIA · LONDON

Published by Running Press,

An Imprint of Perseus Books, a Division of PBG Publishing, LLC,

A Subsidiary of Hachette Book Group, Inc.

Printed in China

Books published by Running Press are available at special discounts for bulk purchases in the United States by corporations, institutions, and other organizations. For more information, please contact the Special Markets Department at the Perseus Books Group, 2300 Chestnut Street, Suite 200, Philadelphia, PA 19103, or call (800) 810-4145, ext. 5000, or e-mail special.markets@perseusbooks.com.

ISBN 978-0-7624-6000-7

Library of Congress Control Number: 2016941583

E-book ISBN 978-0-7624-6110-3

9   8   7   6   5   4   3   2   1

Digit on the right indicates the number of this printing

Cover and interior design by Josh McDonnell

Edited by Jordana Tusman

Typography: Brandon and Hand Gothic

Food Stylist: Mariana Velasquez

Prop Stylist: Richard Vassilatos

Running Press Book Publishers

2300 Chestnut Street

Philadelphia, PA 19103-4371

Visit us on the web!

www.offthemenublog.com

CONTENTS

ACKNOWLEDGMENTS 6

INTRODUCTION 7

A NOTE ABOUT THE RECIPES 14

EQUIPMENT AND INGREDIENTS 16

THE RULES OF THERE ARE NO RULES 19

The Five Categories of Cheese 20

Husk Cherry Compote 28   Spiced Pear Cider Reduction 32

Spring Pea and Sweet Onion Purée 29   Herbes de Provence Caramel Corn 34

Sun-Dried Tomato Pesto 31

Get to Know Your Cheesemonger 36

Fried Pepitas 39   Chipotle Cumin Mustard 42

Lovely Lemon Saffron Marshmallows 40

The Four Main Milks 44

Passionfruit Basil-Seed Curd 48   Herb-Butter Poached Potatoes 52

Coconut Macaroons 50   Smoky Pickled Okra 54

Lactose Intolerance, Dairy Allergies, and Pregnancy 55

Summer Peach Compote 59   Balsamic Rosemary Cherry Mustard 63

Parsnip Purée 60   Rosemary Pine Nuts 65

Coffee Cajeta 62

How Cheese Is Made 66

Deviled-Egg Cream 71   Tomato Caraway Chutney 74

Maple Roasted Apples 72   Laced Balsamic Reduction 76

Affinage 77

Blackberry Honey 80

Brown Sugar Fudge 81

Red Wine Shallots 83

Accompaniments 84

Cardamom Poached Butternut Squash 89

Bourbon Walnuts 90

Dilly Carrots 92

Roasted Cipollini Onions 93

Savory Cherry Chutney 95

A Brief Diatribe on Crackers and Bread 96

Buttered Pecans 100

Stewed Strawberries 102

Smoky Honey Mustard 103

Pickled Fennel 105

Kiwi Mostarda 106

Seasonality 108

Rosé Rhubarb 112

Rosemary Rhubarb Jelly 113

Pink-Pepper Pickled Rhubarb 114

The Benefits and Challenges of Cheese as a Living Thing 116

Baba Ghanoush 120

Sweet and Sour Lotus Root 123

Honeycomb 124

Regionality 126

Spiced Carrot Chutney 131

Sweet and Spicy Red Pepper Jelly 133

Bacon Molasses Mustard 134

Lemon Roasted Asparagus 136

Beverages 138

Carrot Cumin Purée 145

Blood Orange Fennel Chip 146

Anise Meringue 148

Mushroom Duxelles 150

Toasted Walnut Pesto 151

The Occasion 152

Salted Chocolate Graham Cracker 154

Focus and Balance 156

Fava Bean Pesto 160

Spicy Curry Cashew Brittle 162

Shiitake Salad 165

Coconut Pineapple Cajeta 166

Sweet Balsamic Pickled Figs 167

Presentation 168

Castelvetrano Olive Lemon Tapenade 173

Kale Pesto 175

Sweet and Sour Pineapple 176

Golden Cauliflower Purée 178

Green Tea White Chocolate Fudge 179

How to Wrap and Store Cheese 180

Tomato Confit 184

Bacon Love 186

Orange Confit 189

Creamed Corn 190

Sweet and Spicy Apple Chutney 191

Let's Eat! 192

Lush Leeks 195

Brandy Poached Pears 196

Pineapple Mostarda 198

Broccoli Anchovy Purée 199

Sweet Pickled Concord Grapes 201

CHEESE CUTTING GUIDE 202

CHEESE PAIRING GUIDE 204

CONDIMENT PAIRING GUIDE 208

INDEX 214

ACKNOWLEDGMENTS

Special thanks to all the cheese makers who are featured in this book. Thanks to Kiran Lovejoy, Sandra Johnson, Jeff Baker, Dimitri Saad, Emily Lindh, Allen Stafford, BR McDonald, Heather Greene, Adrian Murcia, Karen and David Waltuck, Liz Thorpe, Sasha Davies, Max McCalman, Steve Jenkins, Anne Saxelby, Danny Meyer, Jess Perrie, Ryan Foote, Lynne Eickholt, Pam Alexander, Meredith Erickson, Brad Dubé, Allison Hunter, Kimberly Witherspoon, Lena Yarbrough, Kristen Carbone, Chris Walsh, Chris Sheridan, Tracy Underwood, Allysun Redmond, Megan Johnson, Roman Ramirez, and Katie Geise. Thanks also to the recipe testers and to our generous and supportive families.

INTRODUCTION

"Have you always loved cheese?" I get asked this question a lot, and the simple answer is no. Like most Americans, I grew up eating what was available at the grocery store, from the deli, or in the school cafeteria. I didn't think much about what cheese was or where it came from. The only cheeses I knew were block Cheddar, Kraft Singles, and whatever was on pizza. Other than whatever was on pizza, I knew I didn't like it.

In 2004 I went to work as a server at Chanterelle in New York City, one of the first restaurants in the United States to serve a serious cheese course with dinner. Learning to present the cheese selection to the guests was a requirement of my job. It was also a revelation. Under the guidance of Adrian Murcia, the fromager (a fromager is to cheese what a sommelier is to wine) at Chanterelle, I set out to learn all I could about cheese, and before too long I left to become the opening fromager at The Modern, the fine-dining restaurant at New York's Museum of Modern Art.

At that time, most cheese plates in restaurants in the United States came with one of three things: quince paste, date cake, or Marcona almonds. Each of those pairings can go with *some* cheeses, but none of them goes with *every* cheese. I started to wonder why Americans were stuck in this habit, and I set out to change it. When I opened Casellula Cheese & Wine Café, in 2007, the idea was that we would have a huge selection of cheeses, even better than the selection at most fancy restaurants, and that each cheese would be presented beautifully and paired with an accompaniment that was actually right for the cheese. It's a simple idea; it shouldn't have been revolutionary. But as far as I know, no one else in North America was doing anything like it at the time.

Early on, most of the accompaniments on our cheese plates were store-bought. Mustards, chutneys, honeys, jams, and fruit curds were readily available and pretty good. Then, seven months after we opened, an angel was sent down from heaven to help Casellula reach its full potential. That angel's name was Leigh Friend.

A graduate of the New England Culinary Institute, in Vermont, Leigh had worked as a pastry cook at the famed Gramercy Tavern in New York City. When she was hired at Casellula, she was expecting to make pastries and to help the chef with some savory food. Little did she know that she was about to begin a lifelong love affair with cheese. Up to that point, like so many of us, she'd thought of cheese as an addition to food, something to complement the other ingredients. In the Casellula kitchen she saw for the first time that cheese deserved to be highlighted. She found herself thinking about the flavors and textures of accompaniments that would complement or contrast with particular cheeses, and before long she began replacing the store-bought accompaniments we put on our cheese plates with pairings she made in-house.

I hadn't realized how creative, fun, thoughtful, and exciting those pairings could be. Leigh didn't just replace bought product with the same thing made in-house—she created totally new accompaniments. Over time, I began to see how innovative her recipes were, and how the little things, like adding curry spices to a nut brittle, made a huge difference in the cheese-plate experience. Heck, thinking of serving nut brittle with cheese in the first place was exciting.

Flash forward several years. Late one fall afternoon, I asked Leigh how many different accompaniments she thought she made. She didn't have an exact count, but when we realized that we must serve more than a hundred different condiments with our cheeses, we decided that we should collect some of them in a cookbook. Over the next few months, we worked together to create an outline for what would be a book of condiment recipes, each paired with one cheese, so that readers could just open it up and do exactly as they were told. "This cheese goes with this condiment, and here is the recipe." Done.

But something didn't feel quite right because we don't really work that way at Casellula. We work with dozens of cheeses and condiments at any given time, and each plate is a unique creation—with multiple cheese-and-condiment pairings—that is well thought out by a fromager. Each cheese pairs with multiple condiments, and each condiment pairs with several different cheeses. Each pairing involves many choices, based on the season, the time of day, the beverage being consumed, the other cheeses and condiments on the plate, the mood of the fromager, and the desires of the diner. Sometimes we start with the condiment and pick a cheese, and sometimes it's the other way around.

We also have to make a lot of choices for any given plate to ensure that a broad variety of milks and regions are represented by the cheeses, and then more choices so that we end up with a variety of accompaniments. We may pair a goat's-milk crottin with passionfruit curd on one plate and with white chocolate fudge on the next. We can't just put together a simple list of pairings, and that's what makes our cheese plates so exciting.

For months we worked on a cookbook that would have been easy for everyone to read and understand, but that sucked the life out of our cheese plates. Other than being a collection of recipes, we didn't really know what the book was supposed to be about. So we threw it out and started over. As frustrating as that was, we are grateful for the experience because it forced us to really consider our cheese plates.

The result—this book—is not a traditional cookbook from which you choose a recipe, follow directions, and, voilà, have a completed dish. Instead, the intention of this book is to provide you with the resources you need to create a beautiful cheese plate on your own. Although in these pages we do pair each condiment recipe with a particular cheese, the reality is that each condiment can be paired with multiple cheeses, and each cheese can be paired with multiple accompaniments. The more recipes you prepare and the more pairings you experiment with, the better you will get at choosing interesting, surprising, and exciting cheese and accompaniment pairings for your cheese plate—and the better you will get at creating inspiring cheese plates made up of multiple pairing combinations.

You can spend as much or as little time composing your cheese plate as suits you. If you are a home cook who wants to explore the limitless world of cheeses and learn to create successful pairings and presentations on your own, *Composing the Cheese Plate* will allow you to explore everything from how cheese is made, to how to make a lemon saffron marshmallow, to the fun of developing a relationship with your cheesemonger, to how a jolt of acidity can make a cheese seem less stinky.

If you read every chapter from front to back, which you don't have to do, you will learn the "why" behind the creation of cheese plates so that you will be able to consider the season, your location, what cheeses and produce are available when, how much time you have, and the occasion you are celebrating. Then you will be able to create one-of-a-kind cheese platters, with pairings that you can make from scratch by following our recipes. Your cheese plates will be like no other.

For those of you with less time, or a more, shall we say, measured interest, *Composing the Cheese Plate* makes it possible for you to follow basic instructions and create a solid cheese presentation. Find a recipe you like and pair it with the suggested cheese, and you will almost certainly enjoy the combination. Re-create a cheese platter just as we have in these pages, and it will be impressive and delicious.

Finally, for the time-strapped reader, or those of you who don't care to cook, there are many store-bought products that can be used in place of our suggested homemade recipes. Most quality cheese shops and specialty food stores have selections of compotes, chutneys, jams, fruit curds, mustards, honeys, and pickles, some made specifically to go with cheeses. You can find fudges and brittle at confectionaries, but you may have to forgo flavored marshmallows, for instance, if you don't want to cook them yourself. That's OK, though, as there are plenty of other store-bought options that will allow you to make a perfectly impressive platter while taking up very little of your time.

In other words, you can follow instructions and put together a cheese plate, or you can take the time to compose a cheese plate that is uniquely yours. It's up to you.

—**Brian Keyser,** New York City, 2016

A NOTE ABOUT THE RECIPES

The recipes for accompaniments are intended to be simple and easy to prepare. All of them can be made in advance so you can focus on making dinner or rushing home in traffic, knowing that plating your cheese platter will take only a few minutes. You can certainly make some of the recipes right before serving, but it's probably easier to have them prepared before assembling your cheese plate.

All the recipes indicate how long they should take to make. If you've got very little time to spare, don't choose a recipe that takes hours to prepare. If you can spare the extra few minutes, though, many of the more time-consuming recipes are really special.

Read each recipe from beginning to end a couple of times before proceeding to make it. This will set you up for success every time, ensuring that you don't forget any important steps or ingredients. Have a piece of paper ready to jot down notes for yourself, or, if doing so doesn't offend your sensibilities, write in your cookbook with pencil so you can make changes or notations that suit you.

These recipes are written the way they are for a reason. The order in which the ingredients are listed is the order in which you will use them in the directions.

Many of the ingredients in the recipes are flexible. We recommend making the recipes as written once so that you understand the process and the end result. Then, the next time, make them with a twist, if you wish.

There are occasions when you don't have any time to cook. That's OK. Use our pairing suggestions as inspiration, then go to a good specialty food store, cheese shop, or grocery store, and buy quality retail products. There are dozens of jams, chutneys, fruit curds, nut brittles, roasted nuts, pickles, honeys, and mustards available in stores.

When you have the time, though, you can create something extra special and have fun doing it. Really, most of our recipes will ultimately *save* you time because you will be making items that will serve other purposes—a pesto that goes on your cheese plate will later be used on pasta; mustards and pickles will be reused on sandwiches; brittle will be crumbled onto ice cream sundaes.

Many of the cheeses that we highlight in this book are made in very small quantities and are not widely distributed, so you may not be able to buy all of them at your local cheese shop or market. In those cases we usually recommend more widely available substitutes. In case you are unable to find the substitutes, we give you a brief description of each cheese so that you can ask your favorite cheesemonger for a good alternative in the same style.

Have fun!

—**Leigh Friend,** New York City, 2016

Introduction

EQUIPMENT AND INGREDIENTS

airtight container: We recommend storing each prepared condiment in an airtight container—that is, one with a tight seal to prevent additional air from getting in.

butter: The recipes call for unsalted butter. If salted butter is all you have, please reduce the amount of additional salt used in the recipe, generally by half.

eggs: The recipes are formulated for large eggs, including white eggs, brown eggs, blue eggs, and speckled eggs.

ice bath: Several recipes require an ice bath, an important step for stopping the cooking process instantly. The recipes that require an ice bath note that you should have a bowl of ice reserved in the freezer for this step. Make sure to set it up ahead of time.

large saucepan: Holds about 4 quarts or more of liquid.

measuring cups: When measuring dry ingredients, make sure to level the top with a knife or your hand.

medium saucepan: Holds about 3 quarts of liquid.

micro zester (rasp grater): A specialized grater that zests or grates finely. If you don't have one, you may use a regular zester or grater and chop the zest into fine pieces.

parchment paper: If you bake at all, I highly recommend keeping a roll on hand. It makes baking easy by shielding the baking sheet from burned juices or sticky messes. A lot of the recipes call for a baking sheet lined with parchment paper. If you do not have parchment paper, use a nonstick baking liner or a nonstick baking sheet.

salt: Kosher salt is recommended in all the recipes. It tastes purer than table salt. If you choose to use table salt, please cut the amount in half. Table salt has finer granules, which results in more salt per volume.

silica gel: This is the same substance that's contained in the packets you find in new shoes or clothing. They are used to control humidity. They are not edible, but you can place them in containers holding foods that need to stay dry, such as meringues, brittles, and fruit or veggie chips.

small saucepan: Holds about 2 quarts or less of liquid.

vanilla: Vanilla beans are used throughout the recipes. They can be expensive, but their flavor makes them worth every cent. If you are unable to use vanilla bean, I recommend substituting a few drops of high-quality pure vanilla extract.

THE RULES OF THERE ARE NO RULES

Although we say a lot of things in this book that sound like commands or rules, we actually believe there are no rules. OK, this may be a slight exaggeration because there are a few rules: Never pair a cheese with Skittles or any other accompaniment that is so strong or so sweet that you can't taste the cheese. Never eat spinach that has been recalled by the FDA. Never go up against a Sicilian when death is on the line.

For the most part, though, almost everything we talk about in the cheese world is subjective. There are no right or wrong pairings for particular cheeses. We may love tomato caraway chutney with Chevrolait, and you may hate it. We may think cabernet sauvignon overwhelms most cheeses, but you may feel that if a cheese is wrong with cabernet sauvignon, then you don't want to be right. Our idea of too sweet may be your idea of perfect.

There may be behaviors that are more broadly accepted or issues on which there is broad consensus, but if you disagree with the consensus, then bully for you. The only criterion that matters at the end of the day is: do you and your guests like it? As you read this book and notice when we say this goes with that, or some accompaniment will have some particular effect on such and such a cheese, remember that these are just recommendations and opinions.

We know what you're thinking. Go ahead, send us your cheese-and-Skittles pairing suggestion. As soon as we wrote that sentence, we knew what we were in for.

THE FIVE CATEGORIES OF CHEESE

1. Renaissance Ricotta with Husk Cherry Compote (p. 28)
2. Brillat-Savarin with Spring Pea and Sweet Onion Purée (p. 29)
3. Pecorino Foglie with Sun-Dried Tomato Pesto (p. 31)
4. Hooligan with Spiced Pear Cider Reduction (p. 32)
5. Roquefort with Herbes de Provence Caramel Corn (p. 34)

How do we categorize cheese, and how many categories are there? As with so many topics, there is no single answer. Some cheese professionals like to think in terms of milks. For them, the five main categories of cheese are cow, sheep, goat, buffalo, and mixed. Other cheese professionals consider hardness to be the variable. They may refer to five categories: fresh, soft, semisoft, hard, and blue (although *blue* doesn't refer to hardness). Some may stretch that list to nine, with subcategories including bloomy rind, washed rind, surface ripened, and interior ripened.

At Casellula, we divide our cheese menu into five categories: fresh; bloomy and soft; cooked and pressed; washed; and blue. Is this the "right" way to categorize cheese? There is no "right" way—but it works for our menu. Sure, our categories may be considered a little broad, but they allow room for us to discuss with our guests the differences between, for instance, "Alpine style" and "semisoft," both of which fall into the "cooked and pressed" category.

We acknowledge that no system is perfect. Washed-rind cheeses can be soft and young, or aged and hard; although most are pungent, some are actually pretty mild. Blues come in all shapes, sizes, and textures. If we wanted to put every cheese in exactly the right category, we would have dozens of categories. There's no need for that, so, for the purposes of this book, we are going to stick with the five categories we use at our restaurant.

Fresh Cheeses

Fresh cheeses (see cheese 1 on page 20), as the name implies, are intended to be eaten when young, before they age. They do not have rinds because rinds form over time. They are also the easiest cheeses to make at home.

This is always the smallest category on our cheese menu because many fresh cheeses are meant to be simple. They lack the complexity we seek in cheeses that we are going to highlight on a composed cheese plate. Most cottage cheeses, farmer's cheeses, and cream cheeses, for instance, weren't created to stand on their own. They are primarily ingredients in recipes or vehicles for other flavors. (See page 55 for the one cream cheese that we do love enough to highlight on a plate.) Fromage blanc, queso fresco, paneer, and Halloumi all have their place, and there are some very good ones out there, but we don't generally put them on our composed cheese plates.

That said, there are plenty of delicious fresh cheeses that will be a great addition to your composed cheese plate. Chèvre is goat's-milk cheese made by simply letting the whey drain from the curds through cheesecloth. Ricotta is made in a similar fashion, from cow's or sheep's milk or cream, and can also be made from the whey left over from making other cheeses. Pasta filata cheeses (also called stretched-curd cheeses), such as mozzarella and scamorza, are made by warming milk curds in hot water and then massaging them, stretching them, and forming them into a ball, knot, or roll. In the case of burrata, the stretched curds are wrapped around a center of cream or butter. All of these fresh cheeses can be delicious on their own, used as part of other recipes, or highlighted on a composed cheese plate.

Bloomy and Soft Cheeses

Bloomy refers to the fluffy, white rind that you find on Brie, Camembert, and other, similar cheeses (see cheese 2 on page 20). That white fluffiness is caused by a mold called *Penicillium candidum*. Traditionally, the mold lived in the environment where cheeses aged and appeared naturally on the rind. These days, it is often added to the milk or sprayed onto the surface of the cheese as it starts to age. The white rinds that look "brainy" on some cheeses, such as the one on Coupole, from Vermont Creamery (see page 127), are caused by a fungus called *Geotrichum candidum*.

Bloomy cheeses are generally aged for a short period of time—measured in weeks, not months. They are soft, sometimes chalky, sometimes pliant, sometimes runny. In addition to the well-known Brie and Camembert, you will find other creamy cheeses, like Robiola from Northern Italy and Harbison from Vermont. You can find chalky goat's-milk cheeses like Bûcheron and Chabichou from the Loire Valley, as well as New World equivalents like Crocodile Tear, from Capriole Goat Cheese in Indiana, and Haystack Peak, from Haystack Mountain in Colorado. There are double-crème and triple-crème cheeses, like Mt. Tam, from Cowgirl Creamery in Sonoma, or Brillat-Savarin, from Burgundy (page 20). Humboldt Fog, from Cypress Grove Chevre in California (page 79), has a layer of vegetable ash running through the middle, and Bloomsdale, from Baetje Farms in Missouri (page 108), is dusted on the exterior with vegetable ash.

Cooked and Pressed Cheeses

This is a very large category that gets its name from two tasks that are sometimes employed in the cheese-making process. Curds can be cooked to affect the texture, and they can be pressed to expel moisture. Some of these cheeses are made from cooked curd, some are pressed, and some are both cooked and pressed. These cheeses have less moisture content and are therefore firmer than bloomy and soft cheeses (see cheese 3 on page 20).

Some professionals break this group into smaller categories. An uncooked pressed cheese, like Tomme de la Chataigneraie, is "semisoft," with a spongy texture that gives a little when you push your finger into it. It is very different from cheeses that are both cooked and pressed, like "Alpine" cheeses (e.g., Emmentaler or Pleasant Ridge Reserve), or "hard" cheeses (e.g., Parmigiano-Reggiano or Grana Padano). Although we group all these cheeses into one broad category, we do think about the different types of cheese within it and how they pair differently with accompaniments and fill different needs on the cheese plate.

Washed-Rind Cheeses

Washed-rind cheeses have the bright orange rinds that you may have seen on Époisses, Muenster, or Taleggio. These cheeses are usually (but not always) pungent. In other words, they are what we call "stinky" cheeses (see cheese 4 on page 21). The orange of the rind is caused by a bacterium named *Brevibacterium linens* (usually referred to as *B. linens*).

In most cases, *affineurs* (the people responsible for maturing cheeses; see page 77) wash the exteriors of the cheeses with brine, beer, liqueur, or some other liquid, which prevents molds and fungi from growing but allows *B. linens* to flourish. The bacteria impart a pungent or stinky flavor to the cheese.

These cheeses are not for everyone, but we love them. Some are great on their own, but even the ones that are intensely stinky can be mellowed by the right pairing. Pickles and mustards often do the trick. One of our favorites is pickled fennel (page 97). Certain stinkers can smell downright offensive but become delicious and balanced with a bite of pickled fennel.

This category can include a great deal of variety; it encompasses cheeses that might be cooked and pressed or even blue. Although washed cheeses can be soft, runny, firm, or hard, or small, medium, or large, they can generally be recognized by their orange rind.

Blue Cheeses

Blue cheeses generally contain penicillium mold spores, either naturally occurring or added to the milk. These spores require oxygen to bloom, so the cheeses are pierced, allowing oxygen to get inside the cheese and molds to flourish along the veins created by the piercing (see cheese 5 on page 21).

If you look closely, you will see that some of the "blue" veining is actually green. In fact, many French blue cheeses, such as Persillé du Malzieu and Persillé de Bourgogne, are named after parsley, because that's what the veining looks like.

The blue mold imparts a sharp, strong flavor. Some people think they don't like blue cheeses, but we believe they just don't like them *yet*. If you are one of those people, find a blue cheese, spread it on some bread, and pair it with one of our suggested accompaniments to balance the cheese's intensity. You may just change your mind about blue.

HUSK CHERRY COMPOTE

RENAISSANCE RICOTTA, NARRAGANSETT CREAMERY, RHODE ISLAND
PASTEURIZED COW'S MILK

Husk cherries come out in late fall. Delicately wrapped in a brown, lacey husk, these little gems are bursting with a sweet pineapple flavor. The compote may take a little time to prepare, but we promise you it's worth the work. It also tastes suspiciously like birthday cake. It is a fun addition to this light, decadent ricotta.

YIELD: ¾ CUP
PREP TIME: 15 MINUTES
COOK TIME: 30 MINUTES

1 pound husk cherries (also called ground cherries or gooseberries)

½ vanilla bean

¾ cup granulated sugar

2 teaspoons lemon juice

Remove the husks from the cherries. Rinse to remove some of the sticky residue.

Cut the vanilla bean in half lengthwise with the tip of a paring knife. Reserve half the bean for another use. Scrape out the seeds using the tip of the knife, dragging from one end to the other.

Combine the cherries in a small saucepan with the sugar, vanilla bean, and lemon juice and ⅓ cup water. Over medium heat, bring the cherries to a boil, stirring occasionally. Once at a boil, reduce to low heat.

Once the cherries burst, continue to cook on low until syrupy, about 15 to 20 minutes. Stir occasionally with a heat-resistant spatula. You do not want to caramelize the sugars, so be careful to avoid overcooking.

Once syrupy, remove from the heat and let cool.

Store in an airtight container, chilled.

Chef's note: Make ahead. It will keep for up to 1 month.

Other cheeses to serve with this accompaniment: Bloomsdale, mascarpone, or chèvre.

Creative suggestions: Husk cherry compote will brighten up any yogurt. Or try it as a simple accompaniment with panna cotta.

SPRING PEA AND SWEET ONION PURÉE

BRILLAT-SAVARIN, FRANCE :: PASTEURIZED COW'S MILK

This triple-crème cheese from France is so creamy, fatty, and yummy you will think it's a dessert, which it very much can be. But here we have paired it with a savory purée. (If sweet is what you are looking for, go with the stewed strawberries (page 97) or peach compote (page 55) The purée matches the creamy texture of the cheese, but adds vegetal, aromatic notes.

YIELD: 2 CUPS
PREP TIME: 10 MINUTES
COOK TIME: 15 MINUTES

1 medium sweet onion (e.g., Vidalia)

3 ounces unsalted butter

1 pound fresh peas

1 teaspoon salt

Chop the onion into ¼-inch pieces. Melt the butter in a medium saucepan. Add the onion and peas.

Over medium heat, cook the onions and peas, covered, stirring occasionally, until soft, about 10 to 12 minutes. Do not overcook the peas or they will lose their vibrant green color.

Once the peas and onions are soft, transfer them to a blender. Add the salt. Blend on high until smooth, about 2 minutes, scraping down the sides at least once.

Scrape the pea purée into an airtight container, but don't yet cover it with the lid. Instead, place a small sheet of plastic wrap on the surface of the purée to prevent a skin from forming.

Immediately refrigerate the purée to allow it to cool. Cover the container with the lid once the purée is cool.

Keep refrigerated until ready to serve. Serve at room temperature.

Chef's note: If peas are not in season in your area, you may substitute with frozen peas—but certainly not canned!

Other cheeses to serve with this accompaniment: Vermont Creamery Bonne Bouche, Tomme de Savoie, or young pecorino.

Creative suggestion: Use this purée as an extra flavorful layer in Shepherd's pie.

SUN-DRIED TOMATO PESTO

PECORINO FOGLIE, ITALY :: RAW SHEEP'S MILK

This smooth, gray classic sheep's-milk cheese is made only twice a year. When paired with the rich sun-dried tomato pesto, it creates a spectacular visual. The combination is no less exciting on your palate, where spicy, earthy notes from the cheese and bright acid from the tomato pesto heighten all your senses.

YIELD: 2 CUPS

PREP TIME: 10 MINUTES

¾ cup young pecorino

8 ounces sun-dried tomatoes

1 cup extra-virgin olive oil

½ cup fresh parsley leaves

2 tablespoons red wine vinegar

1 garlic clove

Grate the pecorino on the large holes of a box grater.

Place all the ingredients in a food processor. Blend for 1 minute until combined but not puréed. You want a bit of texture.

Store in an airtight container, and keep refrigerated. Serve at room temperature.

Chef's note: Make ahead. It will keep for up to 2 weeks.

Other cheeses to serve with this accompaniment: Tomme brulée, dry Jack, or Swiss.

Creative suggestion: Toss the pesto with some fresh mozzarella and basil for an unconventional caprese salad.

SPICED PEAR CIDER REDUCTION

HOOLIGAN, CATO CORNER FARM, CONNECTICUT :: RAW COW'S MILK

This reduction is a very versatile accompaniment to many cheeses. We have paired it with Hooligan, from our neighbors at Cato Corner Farm. It is a pretty pungent cheese, but it's delicious. The pear cider provides a kick of acidity and a kiss of sweetness to cut right through that stink. If you need a little more dampening of the funk along with the addition of other textures and flavors, serve the pairing on a slice of fruit-nut bread.

YIELD: 2 CUPS

PREP TIME: 10 MINUTES

COOK TIME: 1½ TO 2 HOURS

½ vanilla bean

½ gallon pear cider

½ cup light brown sugar

1 cup granulated sugar

1 medium lemon

2 sticks cinnamon

2 whole cloves (or a pinch of ground cloves)

2 pieces allspice (or a pinch of ground allspice)

Cut the vanilla bean in half lengthwise with the tip of a paring knife. Reserve half the bean for another use. Scrape out the seeds using the tip of the knife, dragging from one end to the other.

Combine all the ingredients in a medium saucepan. Bring to a boil over medium-high heat.

Reduce the heat to medium. Continue to boil, stirring occasionally, until syrupy, about 1½ hours.

To check for the right consistency, dip a spoon in the reduction and then lift it out.

If the liquid runs right off the spoon like water, you need to cook it a little more. If it is more the consistency of maple syrup, it is finished.

Turn off the heat, and let the reduction cool for 20 minutes.

Strain the reduction through a fine-mesh strainer into a heat-resistant container. Let cool to room temperature.

Keep refrigerated in an airtight container. Remove from the refrigerator 1 hour before serving to soften. Serve at room temperature.

Chef's notes: If you are unable to find vanilla bean, substitute ½ teaspoon vanilla extract, and add it to the reduction just before straining.

Make ahead. It will keep for up to 1 month.

Other cheeses to serve with this accompaniment: Woodcock Farms' Timberdoodle, Cheddar, and so many more!

Creative suggestions: Try brushing some on a roast just as it's finishing, or add a touch to sweeten whipped cream or iced tea.

HERBES DE PROVENCE CARAMEL CORN

ROQUEFORT, FRANCE :: PASTEURIZED SHEEP'S MILK

Popcorn is one of the more popular accompaniments at Casellula. This caramel corn is made a little more interesting with the addition of herbes de Provence, a blend of herbs that comes from southern France—just like the Roquefort. The crunch of the popcorn contrasts with the creaminess of the cheese, and the sweetness of the caramel both brings out the natural sugars in the cheese and plays against its sharp intensity.

YIELD: 3 QUARTS
PREP TIME: 15 MINUTES
COOK TIME: 45 MINUTES

2 tablespoons grapeseed oil or canola oil

5 ounces dry popcorn kernels

½ teaspoon baking soda

1 tablespoon vanilla extract

2 ounces unsalted butter

1 cup light brown sugar

¼ cup light corn syrup

2 tablespoons herbes de Provence

1 teaspoon salt

Over medium-high heat, warm a large stockpot, with the lid on, for 3 minutes. Remove the lid and add the oil. Drop a couple of kernels of popcorn in the pot and cover. Continue cooking until the kernels have fully popped.

Add the rest of the kernels. Shake vigorously, keeping your hand on the lid, for about 5 minutes or until the popping slows to several seconds between pops.

Remove the pot from the heat, remove the lid, and pour the popcorn into a large mixing bowl. Set aside.

Line a baking sheet with parchment paper. Set aside.

Preheat the oven to 300°F.

In a small bowl, mix together 2 tablespoons warm water, the baking soda, and the vanilla extract. Set aside.

In a medium saucepan over medium heat, bring the butter, brown sugar, and corn syrup to a boil. Continue to cook until the mixture has reached 260°F as measured with a digital thermometer, about 5 minutes. Turn off the heat.

Add the baking soda mixture. Stir well. The mixture will bubble a bit.

Add the herbes de Provence and salt, and stir well, about 20 seconds.

Pour the caramel over the popcorn. Stir the popcorn until well coated, and spread on the baking sheet.

Bake the popcorn for 20 minutes, tossing occasionally with a spatula. Remove a kernel and set it on the counter until cool. Test it to make sure it's crispy. If it's still chewy, continue to bake for another 10 minutes. Repeat the test.

When the popcorn is crisp, remove the baking sheet from the oven and set it on a heat-proof surface. Continue to stir the hot popcorn until it's cool, to prevent it from sticking together.

Store in an airtight container at room temperature.

Chef's note: Make ahead. It will keep for up to 1 month.

Other cheeses to serve with this accompaniment: Pleasant Ridge Reserve, Moses Sleeper, or any firm, nutty cheese.

Creative suggestions: Play around with the seasonings. Indian garam masala or pumpkin pie spice are great substitutes for the herbes de Provence.

GET TO KNOW YOUR CHEESEMONGER

1. **Tomme Brulée with Fried Pepitas (p. 39)**
2. **Caña de Cabra with Lovely Lemon Saffron Marshmallows (p. 40)**
3. **Good Thunder with Chipotle Cumin Mustard (p. 42)**

You will learn a bit about cheese by reading about it, but you will learn a lot about cheese by finding a good cheesemonger. Exploit these professionals as the resources they are by talking with them, tasting with them, giving your feedback, and helping them to learn what your tastes are so they can help you find cheeses that you will fall in love with.

Don't be shy. Introduce yourself by name, and learn theirs. If you don't know much about cheese but want to learn, or if you know quite a bit already but want to learn more, it doesn't matter—let them know your leaping-off point. Start by telling them what cheeses you know you like or think you don't like. A good cheesemonger will help you grow in your cheese knowledge.

Unfortunately, some cheese counters are staffed by kind, decent, hard-working people who mean well but don't know what they should about the products they are selling. Meet those mongers and move on. In 2012, the American Cheese Society started offering the first certification of cheese professionals in the United States. Look for mongers who are Certified Cheese Professionals (CCPs). There are also many competent mongers who are not certified, so the lack of certification does not necessarily indicate a lack of knowledge or ability. But if you aren't sure, you can be confident that your monger is a good one if he or she is wearing the CCP pin.

In our experience, the most knowledgeable cheesemongers work in small specialty cheese shops. But there are very good mongers at the cheese counters of Whole Foods, Central Market, Union Market, and other specialty grocery stores and co-ops as well. Shop around as you would for a hairdresser. Find someone you like, develop a relationship, and stick with him or her.

FRIED PEPITAS

TOMME BRULÉE, FRANCE :: RAW COW'S MILK

These fried pumpkin seeds are going to be your friends. Their crunch is great against a cheese like the flaky Tomme brulée, and they are delicious on their own. Sprinkle them around your cheese platter, or serve them in a little dish.

YIELD: 1 CUP

COOK TIME: 15 MINUTES

3 cups grapeseed oil

1 cup pepitas (also known as pumpkin seeds)

Pinch of salt

In a medium saucepan, over medium heat, heat the grapeseed oil to 375°F. If you do not have a clip-on thermometer, check the temperature every 2 minutes using a digital thermometer.

Add ¼ cup pepitas, and fry until they puff up and rise to the surface, about 1 minute.

Carefully remove the pepitas from the oil using a slotted spoon. Spread on paper towels to drain. Lightly sprinkle with salt to season. Repeat with the remaining pepitas.

Store in an airtight container at room temperature.

Chef's note: Make ahead. They will keep for up to 1 month.

Other cheeses to serve with this accompaniment: Chällerhocker, brick cheese, cottage cheese.

Creative suggestions: These are a great garnish for any salad or to add a bit of nuttiness to a yogurt parfait.

LOVELY LEMON SAFFRON MARSHMALLOWS

CAÑA DE CABRA, SPAIN :: PASTEURIZED GOAT'S MILK

YIELD: ABOUT 50 1-INCH MARSHMALLOWS

PREP TIME: 10 MINUTES

COOK TIME: 30 MINUTES

9 sheets gelatin

Grapeseed oil (or another neutral, mild oil)

½ cup confectioners' sugar, plus more for dusting

¼ cup cornstarch

2 cups granulated sugar

½ cup light corn syrup

Pinch of saffron

3 egg whites

Grated zest from 1 medium lemon

½ teaspoon vanilla extract

Place the sheets of gelatin in a bowl of ice water until they are soft, 5 to 10 minutes. Once they're ready to use, remove them from the ice water, and gently squeeze off any excess water. Your gelatin is now "bloomed."

Have your stand-up mixer ready with a clean bowl and the whisk attachment.

Prepare and 8 x 8 inch pan or flexi-mold by very lightly rubbing a bit of grapeseed oil or other neutral oil on the surface with a paper towel or pastry brush.

In a small mixing bowl, combine the confectioners' sugar and cornstarch. Pour the blend into a fine mesh strainer, and lightly sprinkle over the mold or dish to coat. Set aside the prepared mold or dish until ready.

In a medium saucepan, combine the granulated sugar, corn syrup, saffron, and ¾ cup water. Bring to a boil over medium-high heat.

Once boiling, reduce to medium heat, and insert a clip-on thermometer. (If you don't have a clip-on thermometer, check the temperature every 2 minutes using a digital thermometer.) Continue to boil the sugar syrup on medium heat until it reaches 240°F, about 10 to 15 minutes.

While the sugar is boiling, place the egg whites in the mixer, and beat on medium-high speed until soft peaks form, about 2 minutes.

Transfer the egg whites to a clean medium mixing bowl. Return the mixer's bowl and the whisk to the mixer.

Once the sugar syrup reaches temperature, remove it from the heat, and slowly pour it into the standing mixer bowl.

Add the drained, bloomed gelatin.

Slowly turn the mixer to high speed. Beat the mixture until the outside of the bowl is cool to the touch, about 7 to 10 minutes. The syrup will transform into a light marshmallow fluff, with about 3 times the volume of the original syrup.

Once the gelatin mixture is cool, reduce the mixer speed to medium low, and add the lemon zest and vanilla.

Once incorporated, transfer the very sticky marshmallow to the bowl of egg whites, and fold in completely. You will drive yourself crazy if you try to get all the marshmallow out. It's OK if a little is left in the mixer bowl.

Spread the mixture into the prepared mold, and top with a dusting of confectioners' sugar.

Let the marshmallows set at room temperature for at least 6 hours. Cut into 1-inch squares, or get creative!

Store in an airtight container at room temperature.

Chef's note: Make ahead. They will keep for up to 2 weeks.

Other cheeses to serve with this accompaniment: Chèvre or another mild, fresh, soft cheese.

Creative suggestion: Dip the marshmallows in white chocolate for a little delight at the end of a meal.

CHIPOTLE CUMIN MUSTARD

GOOD THUNDER, ALEMAR CHEESE COMPANY, MINNESOTA

PASTEURIZED COW'S MILK

This intense, smoky mustard is a spicy-food lover's treat! Good Thunder cheese is washed in Surly Bender beer, cultures, and salt. The mustard helps to cut through the deep barnyard flavors of the cheese. This pairing is not for the faint of heart!

YIELD: 2 CUPS

PREP TIME: 15 MINUTES

TOTAL TIME: 2 DAYS

¾ cup yellow mustard seeds

¼ cup brown mustard seeds

1 cup white wine vinegar

¼ cup dry white wine (e.g., pinot grigio)

¼ cup light brown sugar

2 tablespoons chopped chipotle pepper

2 teaspoons adobo sauce from the peppers

2 teaspoons cumin seeds

½ teaspoon salt

Combine the mustard seeds, vinegar, white wine, and brown sugar in a 32-ounce jar or container. Let the mustard seeds soak, covered, at room temperature at least 12 hours or overnight.

The next day, add the chipotle, adobo sauce, cumin, and salt to the soaked mustard seeds.

Using a hand blender, blend the mustard until it starts to thicken and hold its shape, about 1 minute. Do not blend too much; you want to avoid breaking apart the seeds and turning the mixture into a purée. (But even if you blend it a little too much, it will still taste good.)

If you are using a stand blender or food processor, pulse the mixture a few times to achieve the desired consistency.

Store in an airtight container, refrigerated. Let the mustard sit for 1 day to infuse the flavors. Serve at room temperature.

Chef's note: Make ahead. It will keep for up to 1 month.

Other cheeses to serve with this accompaniment: Mimolette, Colby, Jack, or English Cheddar.

Creative suggestion: Toss this spicy mustard with pulled pork for a zesty taco filling.

THE FOUR MAIN MILKS

1. Jacquin Chèvre with Passionfruit Basil-Seed Curd (p. 48)
2. Casatica di Bufala with Coconut Macaroons (p. 50)
3. Pleasant Ridge Reserve with Herb-Butter Poached Potatoes (p. 52)
4. MitiBleu with Smoky Pickled Okra (p. 54)

Most cheeses in North America and Europe are made from the milk of cows, goats, or sheep. Therefore, these are the types of cheeses discussed most often in this book. Only a small amount of cheese is made from the milk of the water buffalo, but it can be so good that we insisted on including it, too. Yaks, camels, whales, cats, and other mammals (and the people who love them): please don't be offended by your exclusion.

Cow's Milk

Cow's milk is naturally high in fat, which makes it great for producing cream, butter, and cheese. It is the most common milk used in cheese making because there are more cows and they produce more milk than other dairy animals. The average cow produces six and a half gallons (about fifty-six pounds) of milk per day, but dairy cows, bred for high-volume production, can produce quite a bit more.

In addition to being bred to produce more milk, some cows have been bred to produce milk that is higher in fat and protein, which is better for cheese making.

Cow's-milk cheeses tend to be yellow-orange in color because the milk contains beta-carotene. (The milk from grass-fed cows has much more beta-carotene than the milk from corn-fed cows.) The milk looks white in spite of the beta-carotene because so much liquid is diluting it, but once the whey is removed the orange tint is more concentrated in the solids and thus more visible.

Classic cow's-milk cheeses include Cheddar, Emmentaler, Stilton, Comté, Brie, and Parmigiano-Reggiano.

Sheep's Milk

Sheep's-milk cheeses are less common because sheep produce less milk than cows and take up a lot of space compared to goats. Even though sheep's milk yields a high percentage of cheese due to its high fat content, less milk means less cheese. This makes sheep's-milk cheeses expensive to produce, leading to lower supply and higher prices. But sheep's milk has more fat content than cow's milk, which makes it delicious. The cheeses can be creamy, rich, nutty, and sometimes a little gamy. The best sheep's-milk cheeses have layers of complexity that are rare in other cheeses.

There are a lot more sheep (and better dairy-producing breeds) in Europe than in the United States, so there are a lot more sheep's-milk cheeses from Europe than from the United States. Roquefort, pecorino, Ossau-Iraty, and Manchego are well-known classics.

Goat's Milk

Goats are popular among hobbyists and new cheese makers because they take up very little space and produce a decent amount of milk—six to twelve pounds a day. Plus, nothing against cows or sheep, but goats are curious, mischievous, hilarious, and fun. If you've ever seen anything cuter than a five-day-old goat, please let us know.

Goat's-milk cheeses, at their best, are brightly acidic, clean, and delicate on the palate. The small fat molecules in goat's milk make for easier digestion than cow's milk. If you think you don't like goat cheese, it may be that you've tasted only bad goat's-milk cheeses. We love goat's-milk cheeses of all kinds, but occasionally goat cheese smells like, well, goats, and that can be off-putting to some people. This can happen when the milking does (females) are kept too close to, or downwind from, the bucks (males), who are known for their strong, musky odor. Milk is a sponge for aromas, so one can usually tell if the cheese has been made or stored too close to those stinky billy goats. We suggest that you go to a first-rate cheese counter and ask the monger to give you tastes of some high-quality, clean goat's-milk cheeses. You may find that you do like them after all.

Goat's-milk cheeses come in all shapes and sizes. There are goat's-milk Cheddars, fetas, blues, and Goudas. In addition to fresh chèvre, other classics include crottin de Chavignol, Valençay, Selles-sur-Cher, Bûcheron, and Humboldt Fog (page 77).

Buffalo's Milk

Due to its high fat content, milk from water buffaloes produces the creamiest, cleanest, most delicious cheeses imaginable. That's why buffalo mozzarella is considered such a delicacy. Water buffalo are common in Italy and Asia, but because they produce less milk than cows and can be harder to manage, cultivating them has not really taken off in North America. A few dairies are trying, but as of this writing North American buffalo's-milk cheeses are very hard to find.

PASSIONFRUIT BASIL-SEED CURD

CHÈVRE, FROMAGERIE JACQUIN, FRANCE :: PASTEURIZED GOAT'S MILK

Sometimes it's OK to keep it simple. Passionfruit curd is fresh and tart like lemon curd, but with a unique tropical note. It is delicious with chèvre or any other fresh, rich cheese. Tangy and bright, this combination is a great way to wake up your palate at the beginning of your cheese course.

YIELD: 2 CUPS
PREP TIME: 5 MINUTES
COOK TIME: 20 MINUTES

5 ounces frozen passionfruit juice

¼ cup granulated sugar

2 eggs

2 egg yolks

2 tablespoons butter, cold

Pinch of salt

1½ teaspoons basil seeds

Fill a medium mixing bowl half full with ice, and place it in the freezer.

Pour 3 inches of water into a medium saucepan and bring it to a boil. Then reduce to a simmer.

In a medium heat-proof bowl, combine the juice, sugar, eggs, and egg yolks. Set the bowl over the simmering water. Cook, whisking constantly to avoid scrambling the eggs.

Continue cooking and whisking for 5 to 7 minutes. At this point the liquid should be slightly foamy. Continue whisking until the bubbles are few and the texture has thickened, about 3 more minutes. Be careful not to overcook the eggs; doing so will create an undesirable eggy taste and grainy texture.

Dip a spatula in the curd and lift it out. Run your finger horizontally through the middle of the curd. If the curd holds its shape, it's done. If it runs, keep cooking and whisking.

Once the curd is cooked, immediately transfer it to a blender, and blend on high for 2 minutes.

While the curd is blending, remove the bowl from the freezer, and fill it halfway with cold water.

Carefully add the butter and salt to the blender. Continue to blend on high for 20 seconds.

Place the blender container holding the curd in the ice bath. Stir in the basil seeds.

Once the curd is cool, pour it into an airtight container. Serve chilled or at room temperature.

Chef's notes: Frozen passionfruit juice can sometimes be found in the frozen-foods aisle at an ethnic grocer. Beware that some brands add sugar. If the brand you purchase contains added sugar, reduce the amount of sugar in this recipe to 2 tablespoons.

Make ahead. It will keep for up to 1 week.

Other cheeses to serve with this accompaniment: Bright, fresh cheeses like chèvre, farmer's cheese, or mascarpone.

Creative suggestions: Combine the recipe with 3 cups stiff whipped cream, and pour the mixture into a graham cracker crust. Refrigerate for 2 hours, top with toasted coconut, and you have an easy, light pie.

COCONUT MACAROONS

CASATICA DI BUFALA, QUATTRO PORTONI, ITALY
PASTEURIZED BUFFALO'S MILK

When I met the owner of Quattro Portoni, Bruno, and told him about this pairing, his face lit up in surprise. Coconut and Casatica? Oh, yes! The not-too-sweet macaroons complement the sweetness of the buffalo's milk. Both are delicate and melt in your mouth.

YIELD: 2 CUPS
PREP TIME: 20 MINUTES
COOK TIME: 30 MINUTES

⅓ cup egg whites plus 2 egg whites

8 ounces granulated sugar

¼ cup plus 2 tablespoons smooth applesauce

1 pound unsweetened coconut (also called desiccated coconut)

Preheat the oven to 300°F.

Line a baking sheet with parchment paper. Set aside.

Pour 3 inches of water into a medium saucepan. Bring to a boil, and then reduce to a simmer.

In a medium mixing bowl, whisk together the ⅓ cup egg whites and the sugar.

Set the mixing bowl over the simmering water. Vigorously whisk the mixture until the sugar is completely melted and it starts to get foamy. Continue to cook and whisk for about 7 to 9 minutes, or until pulling out the whisk leaves a "ribbon" on top for several seconds.

Remove from the heat. Fold in the applesauce and coconut until well combined. The mixture will be pretty sticky.

Add the remaining 2 egg whites. Mix thoroughly.

Roll the mixture into ½-inch balls, and arrange them on the baking sheet. If you have a hard time rolling them because they are sticky, dip your hands in cool water, shake off the excess, and continue to roll into balls. Make sure the macaroons do not touch each other.

Bake at 325°F for approximately 20 minutes, rotating once, or until golden-brown. Keep an eye on them. They will burn easily if your oven has a hot spot or if they're overcooked.

Once golden, remove from the oven and let cool to room temperature.

Store in an airtight container at room temperature.

Chef's note: Make ahead. They will keep for up to 2 weeks.

Other cheeses to serve with this accompaniment: Gina Marie Cream Cheese, chèvre, or a mild washed-rind cheese.

Creative suggestion: Dip the macaroons in chocolate and then roll them in cocoa powder to satisfy a sweet-tooth craving.

HERB-BUTTER POACHED POTATOES

PLEASANT RIDGE RESERVE, UPLANDS CHEESE, WISCONSIN
RAW COW'S MILK

Pleasant Ridge Reserve, the only three-time winner of Best in Show from the American Cheese Society, is made seasonally while the cows are grazing on grass. It is one of North America's best, as good as any cheese from the Alps. Potatoes are a classic Alpine pairing—soft, aromatic, and unctuous. In this case, it's the cheese that brings the sweetness.

YIELD: 3 CUPS

PREP TIME: 10 MINUTES

COOK TIME: 20 TO 30 MINUTES

2 sprigs rosemary

2 cups unsalted butter

2 garlic cloves, lightly cracked

5 sprigs thyme

1 tablespoon salt

2 teaspoons black peppercorns

12 ounces baby potatoes, about 1 inch in diameter (such as fingerlings or baby Yukon gold)

Remove the rosemary leaves from the stem. Discard the stem.

Melt the butter in a medium saucepan over medium heat. Continue to heat for 2 minutes.

Add the rosemary, garlic, thyme, salt, and pepper. Cook for 2 minutes.

Carefully add the potatoes. Continue to cook over medium heat, stirring occasionally, for 20 minutes, or until the potatoes are soft but not overcooked. When you pierce a potato with a paring knife, the knife should come out easily.

Remove from the heat and let cool to room temperature.

Remove the potatoes from the butter, and drain well before serving.

Keep refrigerated. Serve warm or at room temperature.

Chef's note: Make ahead. They will keep for up to 2 weeks.

Other cheeses to serve with this accompaniment: Taleggio, Cheddar, or Raclette.

Creative suggestion: These are a decadent side dish that can take a meal from good to great. They can easily be made in advance for a party and popped in the oven before dinner.

SMOKY PICKLED OKRA

MITIBLEU, SPAIN :: RAW SHEEP'S MILK

This pairing is not for food cowards. MitiBleu is a strong, savory sheep's-milk blue from the region of La Mancha. Quick pickling helps to make okra, often slimy, more palatable by maintaining some of its crunchy texture. Enjoy this dish with your Southern friends. They may be surprised that okra can taste so good.

YIELD: 4 CUPS
PREP TIME: 10 MINUTES
COOK TIME: 10 MINUTES
TOTAL TIME: 2 DAYS

12 ounces whole fresh okra

1 cup red wine vinegar

½ cup rice vinegar

½ cup granulated sugar

2 tablespoons salt

1½ teaspoons cumin seeds

1 teaspoon yellow mustard seeds

½ teaspoon whole black peppercorns

½ teaspoon red chili flakes

¾ teaspoon ground coriander

2 teaspoons smoked paprika

With a paring knife, remove the fibrous top tip of the okra. Pack the cleaned, trimmed okra pods tightly into a 32-ounce glass pickling jar. Set aside.

Combine the remaining ingredients with 1 cup water in a medium saucepan. Bring to a boil, stirring occasionally.

Remove the pickling liquid from the heat, and pour over the okra until covered. Immediately place the lid on the jar.

Keep the pickles out until they cool to room temperature. Once cool, store in the refrigerator. Keep them for 2 days before serving to properly infuse the flavors.

....

Chef's note: Make ahead. They will keep for up to 1 month.

Other cheeses to serve with this accompaniment: Ibores, Monterey Jack, or fontina.

Creative suggestion: Bloody Mary, meet pickled okra.

LACTOSE INTOLERANCE, DAIRY ALLERGIES & PREGNANCY

1. **Burrata with Summer Peach Compote (p. 59)**
2. **Cottonseed with Parsnip Purée (p. 60)**
3. **Arpea de Brebis with Coffee Cajeta (p. 62)**
4. **Providence with Rosemary Pine Nuts (p. 65)**
5. **Surfin' Blu with Balsamic Rosemary Cherry Mustard (p. 63)**

Lactose intolerance occurs when a person's body does not produce lactase, the enzyme that allows us to digest lactose, a sugar contained in milk. An allergy, on the other hand, is when a person's body treats something otherwise harmless, such as peanuts, shellfish, or milk, as a pathogen. Lactose intolerance and dairy allergies are two different things, but they share some symptoms, such as intestinal discomfort and bloating, causing many people to think they have one problem when it's really the other.

If you are allergic to milk, you'll need to avoid all dairy, including cheese. Sorry. For the lactose intolerant, however, there is good news. Milk contains lactose, but a lot of cheeses don't. Most of the lactose from milk is lost with the whey in the cheese-making process. In addition, lactose breaks down over time, so most aged cheeses, whether cow, goat, sheep, or buffalo, contain little or no lactose and therefore are not a problem for the intolerant.

Over-the-counter medications such as Lactaid introduce lactase into the digestive tract, allowing for the proper breakdown of lactose, which in turn allows the intolerant to enjoy milk, ice cream, cheese, and other dairy products without suffering.

Some people find that they digest goat's-milk and sheep's-milk cheeses easier than cow's-milk cheeses. This is most likely due to the fact that those milks have smaller fat molecules.

If you have trouble digesting cheese, or dairy products in general, discuss possible solutions with your doctor. Experiment with different kinds of cheeses and different remedies. Maybe you are good with goat or lovely with Lactaid. Most likely you will be agreeable with aged cheeses. Don't assume you can't eat cheese just because you've had a bad experience or two.

The chance of contracting a foodborne illness from consuming cheese is exceedingly small. In fact, you are far more likely to get sick from consuming spinach, peanut butter, or beef. But there are some concerns to be aware of.

Common wisdom, as of this writing, is that pregnant women should avoid raw-milk cheeses and eat only cheeses made from pasteurized milk. According to the Mayo Clinic (a source you'd think you could trust), pregnant women should "avoid soft cheeses, such as Brie, feta, and blue cheese, *unless they are clearly labeled as being pasteurized or made with pasteurized milk*" (emphasis added). The logic behind the statement is that pasteurization has killed any pathogens that could make the mother sick and thus endanger the fetus. This advice is well-intentioned and common, but wrong.

Pasteurization was a gift to the world that saved and improved millions of lives by making milk (and lots of other foods and beverages) safer to consume. In the late nineteenth century, as Europe and North America were transforming from agrarian to industrialized societies, people were moving off farms, where food was easily accessible, to cities, where food had to be brought in.

By the time milk reached consumers in cities from dairy farms, it was sometimes days old and hadn't been properly refrigerated, giving pathogens, if they existed in the raw milk, time to multiply and become dangerous. Pasteurization, invented in 1864, killed the potential pathogens in milk, making it cleaner and safer to drink. In the late-nineteenth and early-twentieth centuries, when refrigeration was rare, pasteurization saved millions of people from getting sick.

Pasteurization, however, is not a magic force that makes milk, cheese, or any other food perfectly safe to consume. It is a process that kills most of or all the bacteria, good and bad, *at a given point early in the process* of transporting food and drink from farm to table. The problem is that some dangerous bacteria, including *E. coli* and listeria, can get into food *after* it is pasteurized. Furthermore, any low-acid, high-moisture cheeses, including but not limited to those listed above, can be breeding grounds for pathogens.

Most of the time, pathogens aren't present in milk or cheese, so there is nothing dangerous to breed, and if the product in question is properly refrigerated (below 42°F), any dangerous bacteria are prevented from growing rapidly enough to become a threat. But when that very rare, perfect storm of pathogen, moisture, and lack of refrigeration happens, it can cause sickness, which can, for pregnant women, sometimes result in miscarriage.

Therefore, pregnant women shouldn't worry about pasteurization, which prevents *most* pathogens from growing *most* of the time; they should eat only cheeses that won't support the growth of pathogens, period.

Hard, aged cheeses (in other words, low-moisture cheeses) are too high in acid and too low in moisture for dangerous bacteria to grow. So whether the milk was pasteurized or not, whether pathogens were present in the cheese at some point or not, and even if the cheese is not refrigerated, these cheeses cannot host dangerous pathogens.

Cheese is a great source of valuable nutrients like calcium, protein, and vitamin B12, so everyone, including women who are pregnant, should eat plenty of cheese. We are not doctors or scientists, but our advice to you, if you are pregnant, is to avoid soft, high-moisture cheeses like Brie, feta, and fresh chèvre, even the pasteurized ones, because, although it's very unlikely, they *can* host pathogens. Instead, eat lots and lots of hard, aged cheeses, especially raw-milk cheeses, as raw milk contains good bacteria. Good bacteria help to create an environment in the cheese that discourages the growth of dangerous bacteria, if any are present. As a bonus, good bacteria are probiotic, so they help to keep your digestive tract working. Bottom line: cheese is good for you and your baby, but we always recommend checking with your doctor before enjoying it.

SUMMER PEACH COMPOTE

BURRATA ALLA PANNA, DI STEFANO CHEESE, CALIFORNIA
PASTEURIZED COW'S MILK

Burrata, which is mozzarella filled with cream, is decadent and heavenly on its own. The acid in this compote cuts the cheese's creaminess on the palate, and the tangy fruit gives you a little something to sink your teeth into. We are reminded of a not-too-sweet peach pie à la mode.

YIELD: 2 CUPS

PREP TIME: 10 MINUTES

COOK TIME: 35 MINUTES

6 medium-ripe peaches

½ vanilla bean

⅓ cup light brown sugar

1 teaspoon grated lemon zest

4 green cardamom pods

Chef's note: Make ahead. It will last for up to 1 week.

Other cheeses to serve with this accompaniment: Spoonwood Cabin feta, crème fraîche, or a mild, sweet, creamy blue.

Creative suggestions: This compote is excellent for breakfast served on toast with fresh ricotta and mint. Or blend it and use it as a glaze for roast chicken or pork.

Using a paring knife, lightly score an X in the bottom of each peach.

Fill a medium mixing bowl halfway with ice; add enough water so the ice floats.

Fill a medium saucepan ¾ full with water, and bring to a boil. Once the water is boiling, gently lower the peaches into the water for 30 seconds. Quickly remove them with a spoon or tongs, and place them in the ice bath. Discard the water.

Once the peaches are cool, use your paring knife to peel off the skin.

Cut the peaches into 1-inch slices and then into 1-inch pieces.

Cut the vanilla bean in half lengthwise with the tip of a paring knife. Reserve half the bean for another use. Scrape out the seeds using the tip of the knife, dragging from one end to the other.

Return the peaches to the pot, and add the vanilla bean and seeds, brown sugar, lemon zest, and cardamom.

Cook on medium heat, stirring occasionally, until the juices are thick, about 30 to 45 minutes.

Remove the vanilla bean and cardamom pods and discard. Cool the compote to room temperature.

Store in an airtight container, refrigerated. Serve cold or at room temperature.

PARSNIP PURÉE

COTTONSEED, BOXCARR HANDMADE CHEESE, NORTH CAROLINA
PASTEURIZED COW'S AND GOAT'S MILKS

Boxcarr started making cheese in early 2015 and caught our attention immediately. This gooey, earthy, elegant little square of cheese will make you forget that Camembert ever existed. The parsnip purée is a smooth, vegetal addition to the creamy cheese. Who needs contrasts when you have complements like this?

YIELD: 2 CUPS
PREP TIME: 10 MINUTES
COOK TIME: 20 MINUTES

1 pound parsnips

2 tablespoons extra-virgin olive oil

3 tablespoons unsalted butter

1 teaspoon salt

Peel the skin off the parsnips and trim the tops and bottoms. Discard the trimmings.

Slice the parsnip into ⅛-inch-thick pieces.

In a medium saucepan, heat the olive oil and butter together over medium heat until the butter is melted. Add the parsnip.

Cover and cook, stirring occasionally, until the parsnips are soft but not caramelized, about 15 to 18 minutes.

Once the parsnips are soft, remove from the heat and combine in a blender with ½ cup room-temperature water and the salt.

Purée the parsnips until smooth, about 1 to 2 minutes. Make sure to scrape down the sides of the blender container.

Store the purée in an airtight container, refrigerated. Serve at room temperature.

Chef's note: Make ahead. It will keep for up to 5 days.

Other cheeses to serve with this accompaniment: Brie, Taleggio, or another soft, savory cheese.

Creative suggestions: Try the purée as a healthy alternative to mashed potatoes, or add some chicken stock and fresh thyme to make an easy soup.

COFFEE CAJETA

ARPEA DE BREBIS, FRANCE :: PASTEURIZED SHEEP'S MILK

Cajeta is traditionally made with goat's milk, but cow's milk can be an easy substitute. The coffee in this cajeta really smooths the pungency of the sheep's-milk washed-rind cheese.

YIELD: 1 CUP

PREP TIME: 5 MINUTES

COOK TIME: 1 HOUR

8 cups whole milk, cow or goat

2 cups granulated sugar

½ teaspoon baking soda

2 tablespoons whole coffee beans

In a large pot, bring the milk and sugar to a boil.

Dilute the baking soda in 1 tablespoon of warm water.

Once the milk and sugar mixture reaches a boil, turn off the heat. Stir in the diluted baking soda. The mixture will instantly rise. Return the heat to low, and cook until it does not rise anymore.

Add the coffee beans. Increase the heat to medium and cook, stirring occasionally, until the mixture turns into a thick, smooth caramel, about 1 hour.

Remove from the heat and let cool.

Store in an airtight container, refrigerated. Serve at room temperature.

Chef's note: Make ahead. It will keep for up to 2 weeks.

Other cheeses to serve with this accompaniment: Hooligan, Miranda, or a nutty, aged cheese.

Creative suggestion: Try playing around with different seasonings such as cinnamon, cardamom, orange zest, or vanilla bean.

BALSAMIC ROSEMARY CHERRY MUSTARD

SURFIN' BLU, QUATTRO PORTONI, ITALY :: PASTEURIZED BUFFALO'S MILK

It sounds like it would be made in San Diego, but Surfin' Blu is, in fact, from Italy, where the makers wash the cheese in local Surfing Hop beer. Most important, it is made from buffalo's milk, so the blue kick rides on a wave of rich creaminess. The mustard is sweet, zesty, and aromatic. When the two are paired, the experience is like getting seriously tubed, bro. Or, as the Italian surfers would say, *"Seriamente tubed, fratello!"*

YIELD: 2 CUPS

PREP TIME: 15 MINUTES

TOTAL TIME: 2 DAYS

1 cup yellow mustard seeds

1 cup balsamic vinegar

¼ cup dry red wine (e.g., pinot noir)

⅓ cup dried cherries

1½ tablespoons fresh rosemary leaves, removed from the stem

⅓ cup light brown sugar

¼ teaspoon salt

Combine the mustard seeds, vinegar, and red wine in a 32-ounce glass jar or container. Let the mustard seeds soak, covered, at room temperature for at least 12 hours or overnight.

Using a paper towel, lightly oil your knife blade with a little olive oil. This will help keep the cherries from sticking to the knife. Chop the cherries into small pieces.

Chop the rosemary into fine pieces.

Add the cherries, rosemary, light brown sugar, and salt to the soaked mustard seeds.

Using a hand blender, blend the mixture until it starts to thicken and hold its shape a bit. Do not blend too much; you want to avoid breaking apart the seeds and turning the mixture into a purée. (But even if you blend it a little too much, it will still taste good.)

If you are using a standing blender or food processor, pulse the mustard a few times to get to the desired consistency.

Chef's note: Make ahead. It will keep for up to 3 weeks.

Other cheeses to serve with this accompaniment: Bleating Heart Cheese Buff Blue or Gorgonzola.

Creative suggestions: Spread it on top of toasted bread with duck confit, or pair it with lamb chops.

ROSEMARY PINE NUTS

PROVIDENCE, GOAT LADY DAIRY, NORTH CAROLINA
PASTEURIZED GOAT'S MILK

These seasoned pine nuts almost burst when you bite into them. Providence is an aged goat's-milk brick covered in a gray rind that is created by the molds, yeasts, and bacteria naturally existing in Goat Lady's aging cave. The slightly bitter, rich pine nuts complement the firm, herbaceous Providence.

YIELD: 1½ CUPS
PREP TIME: 5 MINUTES
COOK TIME: 15 MINUTES

2 teaspoons fresh rosemary leaves (removed from stem)

8 ounces pine nuts (also known as pignoli)

2 tablespoons wildflower or clover honey

½ teaspoon salt

Preheat the oven to 350°F.

Line a baking sheet with parchment paper. Set aside.

Chop the rosemary leaves into fine pieces.

Combine all the ingredients in a mixing bowl. Toss well.

Spread in an even layer on the baking sheet, and place in the oven to roast.

Remove from the oven every 7 to 10 minutes, and toss thoroughly to ensure even browning, making sure to incorporate the nuts around the edges of the pan. Bake until the nuts are a golden-brown color. Remove from the oven and let cool to room temperature.

Once cool, break the mixture into small clusters. Store in an airtight container at room temperature.

Chef's notes: After the nuts have cooled, if you find that they are a little chewy, return them to the oven for a couple more minutes to cook the honey a bit further.

Make ahead. They will keep for up to 1 month.

Other cheeses to serve with this accompaniment: Marieke Smoked Gouda, Zimbro, or Manchego.

Creative suggestion: Pair these nuts with lemon sorbet for a light after-dinner treat.

HOW CHEESE IS MADE

1. Kunik with Deviled-Egg Cream (p. 71)
2. Ricotta Scorza Nera with Laced Balsamic Reduction (p. 76)
3. Winnimere with Maple Roasted Apples (p. 72)
4. Chevrolait with Tomato Caraway Chutney (p. 74)

This is not a book about how to make cheese, but we do think you should know enough about the process to be able to choose the right ones for your beautiful cheese plates. Therefore, we are including this very simple explanation of how cheese is made. If you want more details, or you want to actually learn how to make cheese yourself, there are plenty of books out there on the topic of cheese making.

All cheeses are made in the same basic way. The huge variety among the thousands of different cheeses in the world comes from slight alterations in just a few steps.

Start with milk. There's very little else in cheese besides milk—just rennet, salt, bacteria, and (sometimes) mold. Don't worry: bacteria and mold are everywhere in the environment, and most are good for you, even necessary. The other components are very important, but the bulk of what you eat when you eat cheese is milk. It is usually cow, goat, sheep, or buffalo milk because these dairy animals provide the most milk with the most desirable attributes for cheese (fat and protein content). Technically, cheese can be made from any kind of milk, but if you've ever tried to milk a cat you will understand why dairy animals are preferred.

Separate the curds and whey. This is usually achieved by adding rennet, an enzyme that causes the liquids (whey) to separate from the solids (curds). If you've ever made ricotta at home, you know this step can also be achieved with just about any acid, such as lemon juice or vinegar.

Cut the curd. After the whey is separated off, the remaining curd is a solid, similar in texture to soft tofu. Here, the process is different for each style of cheese. The curd can be cut into tiny pieces or large pieces, cut once or cut multiple times. It can be cut with a knife, a wire, or a "harp." The term *cut* is used loosely here, as sometimes the curd is ladled into molds, bags, or bowls. One way or another, however, it is divided.

Add salt. This can be done at various points in the process. Salt is often sprinkled over the cut curds. It can be thrown in by the handful or dispersed with a spreader, similar to one you would use for fertilizer or sidewalk salt. Alternatively, cheese can be rubbed with salt after it is formed in a mold, or it can be dropped in a saltwater (brine) bath.

Give it shape. Most curds are placed in ring or basket molds that give the cheese its shape while allowing liquid to continue to drain or evaporate off. These molds can be small, huge, round, square, rectangular, or anything in between. Alternatively, curds can be placed in porous bags that do the same thing: allow liquid to drain off and give the cheese its shape. (In the case of fresh cheeses like chèvre and ricotta, *shape* is an ambiguous term.) An exception to this step is found in the pasta filata family of cheeses, which includes mozzarella (page 180). To give these cheeses their shape, the curds are softened in warm water, stretched, and then given form by being tied in knots, rolled up, or otherwise shaped by hand.

Age the cheese. Fresh cheeses are made to be eaten immediately. Otherwise, cheeses are aged. During the aging process, molds may grow on the exterior. (Yes, mold grows on cheese that is in a mold. It's confusing.) The exteriors may be washed (see page 26), allowing for the growth of bacteria. The bacteria in the curds grow and thrive, changing the flavor of the cheese. The cheese may be flipped, to ensure symmetry, or not flipped, to ensure a lack of symmetry. Cheeses may be wrapped in leaves or bark, or they may be covered in wax, as with Goudas, to prevent a rind from forming and to maintain moisture. Blue cheeses are pierced so that oxygen can feed the molds on the interior of the cheese. One way or another, they are matured (see page 77).

There are a few other, optional steps. Milk may be pasteurized or thermalized. (Like pasteurization, thermalization involves heating the milk, but at a lower temperature and for a longer period of time.) Cultures may be added to replace the good bacteria that were killed during pasteurization. Curds may be cooked to affect the texture. After the curds are cut, they may be pressed, to force out moisture. They may be cheddared—that is, stacked, pressed, and then put through a device resembling a wood chipper. Flavors, such as peppers, nettles, or truffles, may be added to the curd or rubbed on the exterior of the finished cheese.

All cheeses have the same basic ingredients and are made following the same basic steps. Simple as that sounds, these few variables result in thousands of different cheeses.

DEVILED-EGG CREAM

KUNIK, NETTLE MEADOW FARM, NEW YORK
PASTEURIZED COW'S AND GOAT'S MILKS

This triple-crème coats the palate with flavors of lemon, butter, and straw. Memories of picnics past should arise when it is paired with the slightly spicy deviled-egg cream.

YIELD: 2 CUPS
PREP TIME: 25 MINUTES
COOK TIME: 45 MINUTES

12 eggs

½ cup mayonnaise

1½ teaspoons dry mustard powder

1 teaspoon onion powder

½ teaspoon black pepper

1 teaspoon hot sauce (e.g., Sriracha)

1 teaspoon salt

Chef's note: Make ahead. It will keep for up to 5 days.

Other cheeses to serve with this accompaniment: Dancing Fern, Camembert, or a bloomy-rind cheese.

Creative suggestion: For a quick breakfast, spread the cream on toast and top with capers.

Fill a medium mixing bowl halfway with ice and place in the freezer.

Gently put the eggs in a medium saucepan, and add cold water to cover.

Over medium-high heat, bring the water to a boil. Reduce the heat to a gentle boil. Continue to cook for 9 minutes. Avoid overcooking the eggs, which results in a gray color on the outside of the cooked yolk.

While the eggs are boiling, remove the ice from the freezer, and fill the bowl halfway with cold water.

Remove the eggs from the heat, and immediately place them in the ice bath. Let chill for at least 20 minutes or until completely cool.

Peel the eggs. Separate the yolks from the whites. Reserve the whites for another use.

Place the egg yolks in a fine-mesh strainer over a small mixing bowl, and push them through using your hand or a spatula. Tap the strainer to remove as much yolk as possible.

Add the remaining ingredients. Mix together until combined.

Let stand for 1 hour before serving.

Keep refrigerated in an airtight container. Serve cold or at room temperature.

How Cheese Is Made

MAPLE ROASTED APPLES

WINNIMERE, JASPER HILL FARM, VERMONT :: RAW COW'S MILK

We love this cheese so much. Get it when it's ripe, peel off the top, and dig in with a spoon. It doesn't need anything else, but it is also great spread on fruit-nut bread and served with these tasty roasted apples. The apples are fun to see on the plate, too. The pairing just screams winter, which is the only time the cheese is available.

YIELD: 16 APPLES
PREP TIME: 20 MINUTES
COOK TIME: 1 HOUR

2 cups maple syrup

2 tablespoons unsalted butter

½ teaspoon ground cinnamon

¼ teaspoon ground nutmeg

Pinch of salt

16 Lady apples or crabapples, peeled

Preheat the oven to 325°F.

In a small saucepan over medium heat, cook the maple syrup and butter until melted and warm, about 5 minutes. Stir in the cinnamon, nutmeg, and salt.

Peel the apples, leaving the stems on if they have them. Set the apples upright in an 8 x 8-inch ovenproof dish.

Pour the maple syrup mixture over the apples. Bake the apples for 45 minutes to 1 hour, brushing a bit of the syrup on the apples with a pastry brush every 15 minutes, until the apples are tender and lightly caramelized.

Remove from the oven and let cool to room temperature.

Store in an airtight container. Keep refrigerated. Serve at room temperature or warm.

Chef's notes: Maple syrup can be expensive, so make sure to use all the syrup in other ways.

Make ahead. They will keep for up to 5 days.

Other cheeses to serve with this accompaniment: Marieke Gouda Premium, Ameribella, or American Cheddar.

Creative suggestion: Serve the apples warm with chopped bourbon walnuts (page 84) and some ice cream or whipped crème fraiche.

TOMATO CARAWAY CHUTNEY

CHEVROLAIT, PRODIGAL FARM, NORTH CAROLINA

PASTEURIZED GOAT'S MILK

This cheese has so much personality, just like cheese maker Kat's 1955 blue Chevy pickup, for which it's named. Packed with umami and radiating an aroma reminiscent of peanut butter, when paired with the tomato chutney it's a savory sensation.

YIELD: 2 CUPS

PREP TIME: 25 MINUTES

COOK TIME: 30 MINUTES

10 ripe plum tomatoes

1 garlic clove

1 small onion

2 tablespoons extra-virgin olive oil

4 teaspoons whole caraway seeds

12 fenugreek seeds

1 teaspoon black sesame seeds

1 bay leaf

3 tablespoons sherry vinegar

1 teaspoon granulated sugar

Pinch of salt

Fill a medium mixing bowl halfway with ice and place in the freezer.

Fill a large saucepan ¾ full with water and bring to a boil.

Using the tip of a paring knife, cut about an inch into the stem end of each tomato, angling inward. Circle the stem with your knife, and remove and discard the core. Cut a small X into the other end of each tomato, about ½ inch by ½ inch.

Remove the ice from the freezer and fill the bowl halfway with cold water.

Gently lower the tomatoes into the boiling water. Boil for 2 minutes. You will see the skin start to peel away where you cut the X's.

Remove the tomatoes from the boiling water, and immediately place them in the ice bath. Once they are completely cooled, remove them from the ice bath.

Using a paring knife, peel the tomatoes. Discard the skin.

Combine the tomatoes and garlic in a blender, and purée until smooth, about 1 minute.

Cut the onion into ⅛-inch-thick pieces. The onion pieces need not be perfectly uniform, but they should be small.

Heat a medium saucepan over medium heat for 2 to 3 minutes or until hot. Add the olive oil.

Add the onion, and sauté until softened and translucent, about 5 minutes.

Add the caraway and fenugreek seeds, and sauté for 1 minute more.

Add the puréed tomato, sesame seeds, bay leaf, vinegar, and sugar. Simmer on low heat until thick, about 1 hour. Stir about every 10 minutes. If the sauce starts to splatter, place a lid on top, slightly ajar.

Once the sauce is thick, remove it from the heat and let it cool.

Add salt to taste. It is important to add the salt *after* cooking the chutney. If you add it during the cooking process, you risk making the mixture too salty once it has reached the desired consistency and become concentrated.

Store in an airtight container. Keep refrigerated. Serve at room temperature.

Chef's note: Make ahead. It will last for up to 2 weeks.

Other cheeses to serve with this accompaniment: Garrotxa, Ben Nevis, or a firm, nutty cheese.

Creative suggestions: Try this savory chutney on top of a warm lentil salad or baked fish.

How Cheese Is Made

LACED BALSAMIC REDUCTION

RICOTTA SCORZA NERA, MARCELLI FORMAGGI, ITALY :: RAW SHEEP'S MILK

This farmstead beauty from the rolling hills of Abruzzo, Italy, is made from the whey of raw sheep's milk. The naturally black rind conceals a pure, delicate, white paste. The balsamic reduction is a great way to make a lot of impact without detracting from the beauty of the cheese. The sweet acidity from the balsamic vinegar cuts right through the sharp sheep's-milk flavor.

YIELD: ½ CUP

PREP TIME: 5 MINUTES

COOK TIME: 1 TO 1½ HOURS

2 cups balsamic vinegar

1 cup granulated sugar

1 pod star anise

4 long strips orange zest (removed from a medium orange with a veggie peeler)

Pinch of salt

Preheat the oven to 325°F.

Combine all ingredients in a small oven-proof saucepan. Mix well. Bake for 1 to 1½ hours, or until syrupy, stirring occasionally.

Remove from the oven and let cool. Remove the orange zest and star anise.

If the reduction is too thick at room temperature, you can add a little hot water to thin it.

Store in an airtight container at room temperature.

Chef's notes: If you are in a hurry, you can boil the mixture for about 15 minutes before placing it in the oven. But beware: your house may smell like vinegar for a day or two.

Make ahead. It will keep for 1 month or more.

Other cheeses to serve with this accompaniment: Parmigiano-Reggiano or another hard, firm, salty cheese.

Creative suggestions: Drizzle over vanilla gelato, or brush a little on your roast just before finishing.

AFFINAGE

1. Humboldt Fog with Blackberry Honey (p. 80)
2. Ossau-Iraty with Brown Sugar Fudge (p. 81)
3. Ameribella with Red Wine Shallots (p. 83)

There are three essential steps to creating a fine cheese, each requiring different skills and resources. The first two are dairy farming and cheese making (see page 66). The third is a step many people don't completely understand: affinage.

According to UrbanDictionary.com, affinage is "The art of selecting, nurturing, and maturing cheese to achieve peak ripeness, superb texture, and genuine flavor." We think that's about as good a definition as there could be, but this is the cheese world (hell, this is the world), so there are many competing definitions. The American Cheese Society calls the process "cheese ripening," the Artisanal Premium Cheese Center refers to it as "refining," and the French translate it as "maturing." It is commonly just called "aging." Regardless of the nuances, though, affinage is what happens after a cheese is made and before it is consumed.

For us, the important concept is "maturing." An affineur takes a young cheese and nurtures it, controlling the temperature and humidity, flipping it at the right times, washing it, piercing it, and so on, until it is ready to be sent out into the world and eaten. The cheese doesn't just need to get older—to "age"—it needs to get better, tastier, creamier or harder, funkier or mellower. Like us, cheese doesn't simply grow older; it matures.

For a fresh cheese, this process is nonexistent. The cheese doesn't age; it is ready for consumption as soon as it is made. For other cheeses, the process can require a few days, weeks, months, or years in a temperature- and humidity-controlled space. We cheese people like to call these spaces cellars or caves (pronounced "cahv," after the French), and in several places, including the Cellars at Jasper Hill Farm in Vermont, Crown Finish Caves in Brooklyn, and Caves of Faribault in Minnesota, affineurs are maturing cheeses in actual caves that are dug out of the earth. But in many places, especially in the New World, caves are, in fact, walk-in refrigerators. In New York City, we get a kick out of visiting affineurs who refer to their "cahvs," which are more likely to be located on the second floor of an office building than dug out of the side of a mountain.

Often, the people who make the cheese also mature it. On many small farms in the United States, all three steps (milking the animal, making the cheese, and maturing the cheese) are undertaken in different rooms on the same farm by the same people. The resulting product is called farmstead cheese. In other cases, the cheese maker passes the cheese on to an affineur, who has the facilities, time, and expertise to age the cheeses. This practice is very common in Europe and is becoming more so in North America.

Whether you think affineurs are the rock stars of the cheese world or just worker bees, and whether or not the affineur and the cheese maker are the same person, the fact remains that cheese must be nurtured from the time it is made until the time it is consumed, and someone with the know-how needs to do the nurturing.

BLACKBERRY HONEY

HUMBOLDT FOG, CYPRESS GROVE, CALIFORNIA
PASTEURIZED GOAT'S MILK

In the same way that you never forget your first kiss, you never forget your first bite of a truly great cheese. For many Americans, this one was it. Block Cheddar and sliced Jack are just pecks on the forehead from your grandmother. Humboldt Fog is a make-out session under the bleachers with . . . well, you know who we're talking about. At the risk of our being crude, the blackberry honey gets you to second base.

YIELD: 2 CUPS
PREP TIME: 5 MINUTES
COOK TIME: 10 MINUTES

1½ cups wildflower or clover honey

3 pints blackberries

¼ teaspoon salt

1 tablespoon fresh lemon juice

Combine all the ingredients with ¼ cup water in a medium saucepan. Over medium heat, bring the berries to a boil. Stir and cook for 5 minutes.

Remove from the heat and carefully pour into the blender. Blend on high for 1 minute.

Pour the mixture through a fine-mesh strainer, pressing on the seeds to remove as much liquid as possible.

Let cool and store in an airtight container. Keep refrigerated. Serve cold or at room temperature.

Chef's note: Make ahead. It will keep for up to 2 weeks.

Other cheeses to serve with this accompaniment: Fresh chèvre, Grevenbroeker, or a mild, sweeter washed-rind cheese

Creative suggestions: Try this blackberry honey on your waffles, pancakes, or anything breakfasty—even in a mimosa!

BROWN SUGAR FUDGE

OSSAU-IRATY, FRANCE :: PASTEURIZED SHEEP'S MILK

This pairing is truly craveable! Salty and sweet flavors from both the fudge and the cheese keep your palate wanting more. The super-sweet fudge is based on a traditional Mexican confection and is paired with one of the great traditional Basque cheeses of France.

YIELD: ABOUT 1½ POUNDS
PREP TIME: 5 MINUTES
COOK TIME: 15 MINUTES

5 ounces evaporated milk

6 ounces unsalted butter

1 pound light brown sugar

1⅔ cups confectioners' sugar

½ teaspoon vanilla extract

¾ teaspoon salt

Chef's note: Make ahead. It will keep for up to 1 month.

Other cheeses to serve with this accompaniment: Vermont Shepherd Verano, Gouda, or a strong, sweet blue.

Creative suggestions: Try folding in some nuts or a warm spice like cinnamon or nutmeg.

Stir together the milk, butter, and brown sugar in a medium saucepan. Over medium heat, bring the mixture to a boil, stirring occasionally.

Insert a clip-on thermometer. Continue to boil uninterrupted until the temperature reaches 240°F, about 15 minutes.

Once the mixture has reached temperature, remove the pan from the heat and pour the fudge into a standing mixer bowl. Do not scrape the bottom of the pan. There will be some burned bits on the bottom. Leave them behind.

On low speed with the paddle attachment, mix for 1 minute. Turn off the mixer.

Add the confectioners' sugar, vanilla, and salt. Turn mixer on low and mix until combined, about 1 minute.

Increase the mixer speed to medium, and continue to mix until the blend is warm to the touch and has the consistency of peanut butter.

Spread the fudge evenly into a 6 x 6-inch baking dish. Place in the refrigerator and chill until firm and cool.

Keep refrigerated. Cut and serve at room temperature.

RED WINE SHALLOTS

AMERIBELLA, JACOBS & BRICHFORD FARMSTEAD CHEESE, INDIANA
RAW COW'S MILK

If you get a chance to taste Ameribella you're in for a real treat. This seasonal cheese is consistently a stunning bright-orange color. At its peak, its flavor is meaty and its texture is custardy, waiting to be spooned out. Like so many washed-rind cheeses it benefits from a splash of acidity. The red wine shallots do the trick while also contributing a little savory sweetness.

YIELD: 1 CUP

PREP TIME: 15 MINUTES

COOK TIME: ABOUT 30 MINUTES

8 ounces shallots

½ teaspoon fresh rosemary leaves, finely chopped

1⅓ cups dry red wine (e.g., pinot noir)

⅓ cup red wine vinegar

⅔ cup granulated sugar

1 bay leaf

½ teaspoon salt

¼ teaspoon black pepper

Peel the shallots and discard the skin. Slice the shallots into ⅛-inch-thick rounds.

In a medium saucepan, combine the shallots and rosemary with the remaining ingredients. Cook over medium-high heat, stirring occasionally, for about 30 minutes, or until most of the liquid is reduced and syrupy.

Remove from heat and let cool.

Keep refrigerated. Serve at room temperature.

Chef's note: Make ahead. It will keep for up to 2 weeks.

Other cheeses to serve with this accompaniment: Smooth, savory washed-rind cheeses like Meadow Creek Grayson or Taleggio.

Creative suggestions: Take this pairing to another level by putting it on a burger or pairing it with pâté.

1. **Rosso di Langa with Cardamom Poached Butternut Squash (p. 89)**
2. **O'Banon with Bourbon Walnuts (p. 90)**
3. **Manchego Añejo El Cortijo with Dilly Carrots (p. 92)**
4. **Chällerhocker with Roasted Cipollini Onions (p. 93)**
5. **Stilton with Savory Cherry Chutney (p. 95)**

The central idea behind our cheese plates is that every cheese should be served with an accompaniment that is right for the cheese. So, although we call it a *cheese* plate, we are just as likely to approach a plate by thinking about the accompaniments first. Ultimately, the goal is to find a combination of flavors and textures that elevates the individual elements on the plate, so that together they create a unique experience in which the whole is greater than the sum of its parts. In order for that to happen, there are a lot of things to consider.

When purchasing or harvesting ingredients for your accompaniments, it's important to start with the best quality available. This does not necessarily mean that you should buy the most expensive ingredients; it means that you should buy the *right* ingredients. We always recommend that you get your produce from farmers' markets when possible (if you aren't growing it yourself), or from the best grocery store you can find. Buy what is in season locally when you can. A tomato picked yesterday fifty miles away is going to taste a whole lot better than one picked ten days ago in a different hemisphere and ripened in a shipping container.

During the spring and summer months, when a variety of produce is plentiful, you will want to use the recipes in this book to preserve the season by pickling fruits and vegetables and freezing purées and compotes. You may even try canning the compotes, jams, and jellies if you are into that. In autumn and winter, you will build your cheese plates by considering what condiments you have at hand and choosing cheeses to pair with them.

Most of the recipes in this book yield more than you will need for one cheese plate. You can save the remainder for another time or use it for a totally different purpose—for example, you can smother your favorite sandwich in kale pesto, or top ice cream with curry cashew brittle. Get creative.

You want to have a variety of flavors on your cheese plate, so think about how your condiments hit the five flavor notes perceived by the human palate: salty, sweet, bitter, sour, and umami. Most of the recipes in this book include multiple flavor notes, providing you with a lot to play with. Caramel corn, for instance, is salty and sweet. Pickles are sour, but some are also a little sweet, and others have a touch of bitterness. Mostardas and mustards can be bitter, sour, sweet, and umami all at the same time. Roasted nuts are salty and umami. Think about the flavor profile of what you are making, and consider how it will complement or contrast with a particular cheese. Combining flavor notes on one plate will both make your plates more interesting and cause your taste buds to rejoice.

We use a lot of acidic ingredients in our recipes—for example, tomatoes, lemon juice, vinegar, and olives. Acid pairs very well with cheese because it pulls the fat off your palate as you eat. Acid brightens deeper flavors and helps to cut through strong ones. The stronger the flavor of the cheese, the better a high-acid accompaniment will work with it.

We especially like to pair very acidic accompaniments, like pickles, with very stinky cheeses. Acid also balances out the saltiness of the cheese. Try the following technique if you put too much salt in a dish you are making at home: add more tomatoes or a touch of red wine to oversalted minestrone soup, or squeeze a lime into oversalted guacamole. You can never take the salt back, but the acid will help to balance it out. The same principle can be applied to something overly sweet. In the Summer Peach Compote, on page 59, we use lemon to brighten the peach flavor that can get lost in the cooking process.

We always consider contrasting versus complementing flavors, textures, and appearances and try to do a little of both. Consider the platter pictured on page 89. The chalky, milky, white O'Banon is contrasted in flavor, texture, and appearance by the dark, crunchy, bittersweet bourbon walnuts. The pickled carrots and butternut squash make the loudest visual statement, complementing the Rosso di Langa with their orange hues. Most of the pairings offer contrasts in flavors and textures, but the chällerhocker and the roasted cipollini onions are both earthy, savory studies in umami, intensifying each other with their complementary flavors.

Our favorite contrast is salty/sweet, which you can get in one item, such as salted chocolate graham crackers (page 152), or by combining two items, such as herbes de Provence caramel corn with salty Roquefort (page 21). Keep in mind that you do not want your accompaniments to be too salty. Cheese contains quite a bit of salt already, which the accompaniments are meant to complement. Nor do you want them to be too sweet, as sugar can overwhelm the palate, making it hard to fully appreciate other flavors. Sweetness tends to be very craveable, and that's a good thing, but it's all about balance.

In addition to flavor, texture plays an important part in the pairing experience. A soft condiment, like fudge or a purée, has a very different effect on your palate than does a hard brittle or a crisp vegetable. In general, hard cheeses pair well with hard textures that crunch, such as a nut brittle or caramel corn. A delicate, smooth purée can taste good with a hard cheese, but the flavor may dissipate by the time the true taste of the cheese coats your palate. Soft cheeses have a little more room for play. Soft textures like fudge and fruit curd complement the cheese, while crisp pickles or crunchy nuts offer a pleasant contrast.

You never get a second chance to make a first impression, and your guests' first impression of your cheese plate is going to be visual. When choosing accompaniments for cheeses, consider how the color, shape, and visual texture will look with a particular cheese, against a particular surface, and with the other accompaniments on the platter. A little visual excitement is great on a plate, but you don't need every pairing to be bright or flashy. If you think that something looks drab, garnish it with a splash of color, as we do by sprinkling chopped chives on creamed corn (page 180). Mix up the visuals on your plate with neutral tones here and a jolt of vivacity there.

Any one cheese will pair well with several different accompaniments of different styles for different reasons. A sweet candy may contrast with the salty bitterness of a particular cheese, while a pickle cuts through it, and a pesto complements it. You never have to worry about repeating similar accompaniments on a plate because you always have options (see our pairing lists on page 204). At the restaurant, we like to have three or four very different condiments that we know will pair well with each cheese.

We hope to inspire you to make the recipes in this book as they are, but feel free to use what's in your fridge or cabinets. Browse the shelves at your local market as well. You may find yourself inspired by something grown right next door. In most recipes you can easily make quick substitutions with what you have at hand, like using frozen corn when fresh is unavailable. Everyone's palate is different—that's why the gods made chocolate *and* vanilla. It is OK if not everyone who eats from your cheese plate likes every pairing you've chosen. You won't like every pairing you've chosen, either! But when you get it right, most people will like most of your pairings and will love a lot of them. Discussing opinions about the pairings is part of the experience. Remember, sharing a cheese plate should be social.

Take a deep breath, and accept the fact that you do not know if a combination will work until you try it. That should be part of the fun!

CARDAMOM POACHED BUTTERNUT SQUASH

ROSSO DI LANGA, ALTA LANGA, ITALY
PASTEURIZED COW'S AND SHEEP'S MILKS

Cheese is sexy. Come on, admit it. The glistening, sugary, spiced butternut squash paired with the charming annatto-washed Rosso di Langa is like that hot dream you wish would never end.

YIELD: 4 CUPS
PREP TIME: 15 MINUTES
COOK TIME: 30 MINUTES

1 medium butternut squash

½ medium lemon

½ vanilla bean

2 tablespoons whole green cardamom pods

6 cups granulated sugar

½ teaspoon salt

Chef's note: Make ahead. It will keep for up to 2 weeks.

Other cheeses to serve with this accompaniment: Cottage cheese, chèvre, or a mild washed-rind cheese.

Creative suggestions: Chop up the squash and mix it with rice or tapioca pudding for an exotic flavor.

Peel the butternut squash using a vegetable peeler. Cut the top and bottom off the squash and discard. Cut the squash in half lengthwise. Using a spoon, scoop out the seeds and discard. Set the squash cut-side down on a cutting board, and slice into ¼-inch-thick pieces. Set aside.

Using the vegetable peeler, peel the zest from half a lemon into long strips. Reserve the rest of the lemon for another use.

Cut the vanilla bean in half lengthwise with the tip of a paring knife. Reserve half the bean for another use. Scrape out the seeds using the tip of the knife, dragging from one end to the other.

In a medium saucepan, stir together the lemon zest, vanilla bean and seeds, cardamom pods, sugar, salt, and 5 cups of water. Bring to a boil, and boil for 1 minute.

Reduce the heat to a simmer. Gently lower the squash into the poaching liquid. Poach the squash, stirring gently every 15 minutes, for about 30 to 45 minutes. The squash should be soft but not overcooked. When you pierce the squash with a paring knife, it should come out easily.

Once the squash is soft, remove it from the heat and let cool in the refrigerator.

Once cool, gently transfer the squash with a slotted spoon to an airtight container. Pour the poaching liquid over the squash to cover.

Keep refrigerated. Serve at room temperature.

Accompaniments

BOURBON WALNUTS

O'BANON, CAPRIOLE GOAT CHEESE, INDIANA :: PASTEURIZED GOAT'S MILK

This fresh chèvre is wrapped in bourbon-soaked maple leaves. The bourbon in the walnuts ties them to the cheese, while the bitterness and crunch of the nuts offer a great contrast to the cheese's pillowy-smooth texture.

YIELD: 2 CUPS
PREP TIME: 5 MINUTES
COOK TIME: 25 MINUTES

2 cups walnut pieces

½ cup light brown sugar

3 tablespoons bourbon

3 tablespoons unsalted butter

¼ teaspoon ground cinnamon

Pinch of ground cloves

Pinch of kosher salt

Preheat the oven to 350°F.

Line a baking pan with parchment paper. Set aside.

Combine all ingredients plus 2 tablespoons of room-temperature water in a medium pot. Bring to a boil, reduce heat to medium, and simmer for about 10 minutes, or until the sugar starts to thicken.

Remove the nuts from the heat and spread evenly on the baking sheet. Bake for about 15 minutes, or until the sugar has almost completely thickened.

Remove from the oven and place on a heat-proof surface. With a heat-resistant spatula, toss the nuts until they cool, about 5 minutes. While you are tossing them, they will start to crystalize and separate. Don't worry, this is what should happen.

Once cool, store in an airtight container.

Chef's note: Make ahead. They will keep for up to 2 months.

Other cheeses to serve with this accompaniment: Tomme brulée, a nutty firm cheese, or Stilton.

Creative suggestions: These are great tossed into salads or chopped up and sprinkled over baked fruit.

DILLY CARROTS

MANCHEGO AÑEJO, EL CORTIJO, SPAIN :: RAW SHEEP'S MILK

It's hard not to find a Manchego lover these days. Most have come to adore the nutty, approachable cheese, not even realizing that it's made from sheep's milk. The extra-virgin olive oil in these dilly carrots adds a bit more character. Find a rich Spanish olive oil if you are doing an all-Spanish plate.

YIELD: 4 CUPS
PREP TIME: 30 MINUTES
COOK TIME: 20 MINUTES
TOTAL TIME: 2 DAYS

12 ounces baby carrots

1 garlic clove

Pinch plus 1 teaspoon salt

⅓ cup white wine vinegar

½ cup extra-virgin olive oil

½ teaspoon onion powder

¼ cup fresh dill

Fill a large mixing bowl halfway with ice and set it in the freezer.

Remove the carrot tops and lightly peel the carrots.

Bring a large saucepan of water to a boil. Add a healthy pinch of salt.

Add the carrots to the boiling water. Cook until the carrots are tender throughout but not overcooked, about 4 to 5 minutes.

While the carrots are cooking, remove the bowl from the freezer and fill halfway with cold water.

Once the carrots are tender, immediately remove them from the heat and set in the ice bath to chill.

Remove the chilled carrots and spread on a towel to dry.

Using the flat side of the blade of a chef's knife, press down on the garlic clove to crush the bulb.

In a large plastic bag, combine the crushed garlic, the carrots, the rest of the salt, and the remaining ingredients. Seal the bag, removing as much air as possible.

Let the carrots marinate for 2 days in the refrigerator to infuse flavors. Turn the bag occasionally to blend the ingredients.

Chef's note: Make ahead. They will keep for up to 2 weeks.

Other cheeses to serve with this accompaniment: Red Hawk, Bleu des Basques, or a sharp, aged goat's-milk cheese.

Creative suggestions: Chop these up to add to a grain or bean salad with shaved Manchego on top. They are also great as a mid-day snack.

ROASTED CIPOLLINI ONIONS

CHÄLLERHOCKER, SWITZERLAND :: THERMALIZED COW'S MILK

Chällerhocker is a consistently delicious, savory, washed-rind Alpine cheese that is usually available at only the best cheese counters. It's worth going out of your way to find. When roasted, cipollini onions turn sweet and pair perfectly against the nuttiness of the smooth paste of the cheese, while enhancing its dirty, earthy character. Think French onion soup without the soup.

YIELD: 2 CUPS

PREP TIME: 10 MINUTES

COOK TIME: ABOUT 30 MINUTES

1 pound cipollini onions

3 sprigs fresh thyme

3 tablespoons extra-virgin olive oil

1 teaspoon salt

¼ teaspoon black pepper

Preheat the oven to 375°F.

Line a baking sheet with parchment paper. Set aside.

Using a paring knife, peel the onions. Place them in a medium mixing bowl. Discard the peelings.

Remove the leaves of thyme from the stem and discard the stem. Add the thyme, oil, salt, and pepper to the onions.

Toss the onions well to coat evenly.

Spread the onions evenly on the baking sheet, and bake for 25 to 35 minutes, turning halfway through. The onions should be lightly caramelized on the outside and soft and tender in the center. Once the onions are soft, remove them from the oven and let cool to room temperature.

Keep in the refrigerator. Serve at room temperature.

Chef's notes: You may use pearl onions if cipollini are unavailable.

Make ahead. They will keep for up to 5 days.

Other cheeses to serve with this accompaniment: Quicke's Mature Cheddar, Alemar Good Thunder, or a strong Alpine cheese.

Creative suggestions: Throw these onions into a potato salad, or add them to roasted Brussels sprouts and top with bacon.

SAVORY CHERRY CHUTNEY

STILTON, COLSTON BASSETT, ENGLAND :: RAW COW'S MILK

Sometimes you want to be cutting edge; other times you want to stick with the classic. First made in the early eighteenth century, Stilton is one of the great traditional blue cheeses of the world. The British like to drink port wine with it, and we think the cherry chutney complements the cheese similarly. It's a little tart, a little tangy, but with more spicy and savory notes.

YIELD: 2 CUPS
PREP TIME: 10 MINUTES
COOK TIME: 45 MINUTES

7 pods star anise

1 small sweet onion

1 pound dried sour cherries

1 cup rice vinegar

½ cup granulated sugar

1 teaspoon salt

Grated zest from ½ lime

Place the star anise in a 6 x 6-inch piece of cheesecloth. Tie closed with twine and set aside.

Cut the onion into ⅛-inch-thick pieces. The onions need not be perfectly uniform in size, but they should be small.

In a medium saucepan, bring 2 cups water to a boil. Add the onion and cook until translucent, about 15 minutes.

Remove the onions from the heat and strain through a fine-mesh strainer. Put the onions back in the pot, and add ½ cup water, the star anise (in the cheesecloth pouch), and the remaining ingredients.

Cook the cherry mixture on medium heat, stirring occasionally, until most of the liquid has evaporated, about 10 minutes.

Remove from the heat. Remove the star anise.

Place a quarter of the cherries in the blender, and purée on high until smooth, adding a bit of the cooking liquid if necessary, about 2 minutes.

Transfer the puréed cherries back into the saucepan and stir to combine.

Store the chutney in an airtight container and chill. Keep refrigerated. Serve at room temperature.

Chef's note: Make ahead. It will keep for up to 2 weeks.

Other cheeses to serve with this accompaniment: Ameribella, fontina, or a savory blue.

Creative suggestion: Sweet or spicy salamis pair well with this chutney.

A BRIEF DIATRIBE ON CRACKERS AND BREAD

1. Up in Smoke with Buttered Pecans (p. 100)
2. La Tur with Stewed Strawberries (p. 102)
3. Mimolette with Smoky Honey Mustard (p. 103)
4. Ouleout with Pickled Fennel (p. 105)
5. Ewe's Blue with Kiwi Mostarda (p. 106)

Often when I tell people that I have a cheese-focused restaurant, they ask me, "Do you serve the cheese, like, with crackers?" They phrase it just like that, as sort of a question, sort of an uncertain statement, clearly seeking comfort. In other words, "Please, please, please tell me that you serve the cheese with crackers, because that's the only way cheese is familiar to me. Without crackers, I have no foundation. I am untethered. I am lost in the world."

This question has never made sense to me. Why would *all* cheeses require crackers? Certainly some soft cheeses benefit from the contrasting texture of a crisp cracker. But a wedge of Emmentaler on a Triscuit I do not understand. It is not 1952, and this is not an issue of *Better Homes and Gardens*.

At Casellula, we serve crackers with cheese when it makes sense to do so. We *pair* crackers with cheeses, and when we do so we pair *specific* crackers with *specific* cheeses. A smoked ricotta is made more interesting and comforting on a homemade graham cracker. Pecorino ginepro is perfectly contrasted by a sesame tuile. We don't just throw a basket of Wheat Thins on the table.

When we were first opening Casellula, a similar conversation happened around bread. I argued that we should treat bread the same way we treat anything else that goes with cheese: we should pair it deliberately and selectively. Sure, an intense and creamy blue is mellowed and sweetened by a slice of raisin nut bread, but what on earth does a ten-year-old Cheddar want from a sourdough baguette?

The bread battle I lost. Americans expect bread with their cheese, and when they don't get it they think we've made not a choice but an egregious mistake. They get offended and accusatory. So we have to serve sliced bread with all our cheese plates.

There are many people who put every cheese onto a piece of bread before biting into it, as if cheese cannot be consumed on its own. I cringe when I see it happen, but I have had to learn to accept it.

That doesn't mean I have to encourage it. Instead, I encourage you, sophisticated reader, to try your cheese without bread. Just be open to the idea. And when you do put your cheese on bread or a cracker, do so deliberately. *Consider* what you are doing. If you can't explain to yourself (or to me) why you are doing it—in other words, if the cheese isn't made better by the bread or cracker—then you probably shouldn't be doing it.

A Brief Diatribe on Crackers and Bread

BUTTERED PECANS

UP IN SMOKE, RIVER'S EDGE, OREGON :: PASTEURIZED GOAT'S MILK

We don't always love smoked cheeses, but this one from River's Edge gets the balance just right. Tangy and fresh goat's-milk cheese is mellowed and intensified with smoke, but not too much. It is then wrapped in smoked, bourbon-bathed maple leaves. The cheese is from Oregon, but the smoke makes it feel all Southern, with the buttered pecans causing you to reckon that a whiskey is in order, too. Y'all might try these pecans with other smoked cheeses for the same effect.

YIELD: 2 CUPS
PREP TIME: 5 MINUTES
COOK TIME: 20 MINUTES
TOTAL TIME: 2 DAYS

For the vanilla salt:

½ vanilla bean (you may also use half a vanilla bean that has been scraped of its seeds, left over from another use)

2 cups salt

For the buttered pecans:

2 cups whole pecans

2 tablespoons unsalted butter, at room temperature

3 tablespoons light brown sugar

1¼ teaspoons vanilla salt

Make the vanilla salt: In an airtight container, bury the vanilla bean in the 2 cups of salt. Let stand for at least 2 days to infuse.

Make the buttered pecans: Preheat the oven to 325°F.

Line a baking sheet with parchment paper. Spread the pecans evenly on the baking sheet. Pinch off pieces of the butter and rub it on the pecans. Sprinkle the brown sugar and vanilla salt over the top.

Bake the pecans for 5 minutes. Remove from the oven and toss with a heat-resistant spatula.

Bake for 10 more minutes. Remove from the oven and toss again. The nuts should be dark and toasted but not burned.

Let cool. Store in an airtight container at room temperature.

Chef's notes: Making vanilla salt is a great way to take an expensive vanilla bean to its full potential, especially if you use a bean left over from another use (referred to as vanilla bean scrap). The salt absorbs the warm flavor and aroma of the vanilla. And using vanilla salt is a convenient way to avoid adding moisture (in the form of vanilla extract) to a recipe like this one.

Make ahead. The vanilla salt will keep indefinitely. The pecans will keep for up to 2 weeks.

Other cheeses to serve with this accompaniment: Mascarpone, Idiazabal, or Edam.

Creative suggestion: Make twice-baked sweet potatoes and top them with chopped buttered pecans.

STEWED STRAWBERRIES

LA TUR, ALTA LANGA, ITALY

PASTEURIZED COW'S, GOAT'S, AND SHEEP'S MILKS

These stewed strawberries will quickly become a favorite pairing for lots of soft cheeses and desserts. This delicious mixed-milk "cupcake" of cheese from Italy is what we call a gateway cheese. If you know folks who think they don't like cheese, throw this combo in front of them and watch them ask for more. La Tur is widely available. Paired with the stewed strawberries, it will remind you of unsweetened cheesecake.

YIELD: 2 CUPS
PREP TIME: 10 MINUTES
COOK TIME: 20 MINUTES

2 pounds strawberries

½ vanilla bean

¾ cup granulated sugar

2 tablespoons fresh lemon juice

Chef's notes: If you are unable to find vanilla bean, you may substitute ½ teaspoon vanilla extract. Add it at the end of the recipe.

Make ahead. They will keep for up to 1 week.

Other cheeses to serve with this accompaniment: Ricotta salata, mascarpone, or a mild, sweet blue.

Creative suggestion: Try adding other berries—for example, blackberries, blueberries, or raspberries.

Use a paring knife to remove the stems from the strawberries. Discard the stems.

Cut 1 pound of the strawberries in half lengthwise, and place them in a medium saucepan.

Cut the vanilla bean in half lengthwise. Reserve half the bean for another use. Scrape out the seeds using the tip of the paring knife, dragging it from one end to the other.

Add the vanilla bean, sugar, and lemon juice to the saucepan. Cook the strawberries over medium heat, stirring occasionally, for 12 to 15 minutes, or until they are soft and falling apart.

Turn off the heat and remove the vanilla bean. Discard the bean.

Transfer the cooked strawberries to a blender. Blend on high for 2 minutes.

Set a fine-mesh strainer over the top of the saucepan. Pour the sauce from the blender through the strainer into the saucepan. Discard the seeds left from straining.

If the remaining strawberries are large, cut them in half or quarters. Add them to the sauce. Cook over medium heat for 5 to 7 minutes, or until the sauce is hot but not boiling. Stir often to ensure even cooking.

Once the sauce is hot and has coated the strawberries, remove from the heat. Cool to room temperature.

Store in an airtight container. Keep refrigerated. Serve at room temperature.

SMOKY HONEY MUSTARD

EIGHTEEN-MONTH MIMOLETTE, FRANCE
PASTEURIZED COW'S MILK

Mimolette is a fun cheese. Its exterior looks sort of like a cantaloupe (see page 96), and, well, so does its interior. The dark orange color is imparted by annatto, a seed used as a natural food coloring, and the pockmarked rind is the work of cheese mites. (There's a conversation starter!) When it's aged, as this one is, it can be as hard as a rock, with crunchy crystals and an intense savory, salty flavor. The mustard punches up the savory notes with smoke and balances them with the honey's subtle sweetness.

YIELD: 2 CUPS

PREP TIME: 15 MINUTES

TOTAL TIME: 2 DAYS

¾ cup yellow mustard seeds

¼ cup brown mustard seeds

1 cup white wine vinegar

¼ cup dry white wine (e.g., pinot grigio)

¼ cup wildflower or clover honey

3½ teaspoons smoked paprika

½ teaspoon salt

Combine the mustard seeds, vinegar, white wine, and honey in a 32-ounce glass jar or metal or plastic container. Let the mustard seeds soak, covered, at room temperature for at least 12 hours or overnight.

The next day, add the paprika and salt to the soaked mustard seeds.

Using a hand blender, blend the mixture until it starts to thicken and hold its shape, about 1 minute. Do not blend for too long; you want to avoid breaking apart the seeds and turning the mixture into a purée. (But even if you blend it a little too much, it will still taste good.)

If you are using a standing blender or food processor, pulse the mustard a few times to reach the desired consistency.

Let the mustard sit for 1 day to infuse flavors. Store in an airtight container in the refrigerator. Serve at room temperature.

....

Chef's note: Make ahead. It will keep for up to 1 month.

Other cheeses to serve with this accompaniment: Beecher's Flagship, or Jasper Hill Farm Alpha Tolman.

Creative suggestion: Blend the mustard with olive oil and extra vinegar to make a different kind of honey-mustard dressing.

PICKLED FENNEL

OULEOUT, VULTO CREAMERY, NEW YORK :: RAW COW'S MILK

Pickled fennel may not sound like anything special, but from our point of view it's magic. We've never tasted a washed-rind cheese that wasn't made better by it. When the fennel's sharp acid, subtle sweetness, and aromatics combine with the cheese's creamy umami and bitter notes, the result is a perfect balance of flavors.

YIELD: 4 CUPS

PREP TIME: 10 MINUTES

COOK TIME: 10 MINUTES

TOTAL TIME: 2 DAYS

2 medium fennel bulbs

2 garlic cloves

1 cup white wine vinegar

½ cup rice vinegar

½ cup granulated sugar

2 tablespoons salt

1½ teaspoons yellow mustard seeds

½ teaspoon whole black peppercorns

½ teaspoon red chili flakes

1 teaspoon whole fennel seeds

Cut the tops off the fennel bulbs, and reserve for making stock. Cut the fennel bulbs in half lengthwise. Using the tip of a knife, cut an upside down V in the core on the bottom of each half bulb. Remove the core and discard. Slice the fennel into ⅛-inch-thick slices. Place the slices in a 32-ounce glass pickling jar. Set aside.

Using the flat side of the blade of a chef's knife, crush the garlic cloves. Place them in a saucepan with 1 cup of water and the remaining ingredients.

Bring the pickling liquid to a boil, stirring occasionally.

Remove the liquid from the heat and pour over the fennel until covered. Immediately place the lid on the jar while the contents are still hot. Allow the pickles to cool to room temperature.

Once cool, store in the refrigerator. Refrigerate for 2 days before serving to properly infuse the flavors.

Chef's note: Make ahead. They will keep for up to 1 month.

Other cheeses to serve with this accompaniment: Spoonwood Cabin Cuvette, Jasper Hill Farm Willoughby, or Muenster.

Creative suggestion: As with a lot of our accompaniments, this one is a great addition to a sandwich.

KIWI MOSTARDA

EWE'S BLUE, OLD CHATHAM SHEEPHERDING COMPANY, NEW YORK
PASTEURIZED SHEEP'S MILK

This tart and spicy mostarda will be a favorite staple to have around. It gives any plate a burst of vibrant green speckled with those tiny, crunchy, jet-black seeds. The bright, fruity bite of the Ewe's Blue pairs perfectly.

YIELD: 2 CUPS

PREP TIME: 10 MINUTES

COOK TIME: 1 HOUR PLUS 30 MINUTES

TOTAL TIME: 4 DAYS

1 pound ripe kiwis (about 8 fruit)

1 cup plus 2 tablespoons granulated sugar

¼ cup orange juice

½ cup dry white wine (e.g., pinot grigio)

1 tablespoon dry mustard powder

Chef's note: Make ahead. It will keep for up to 1 month in the fridge.

Other cheeses to serve with this accompaniment: A sheep's-milk blue or a fruity washed rind.

Creative suggestion: Use this mostarda as a marinade for grilled pork or pineapple.

Peel the kiwis and cut into 1-inch pieces.

Toss together the kiwis, sugar, and orange juice in a medium mixing bowl. Transfer the fruit to a heat-proof container and let sit in the refrigerator for at least 12 hours or overnight.

The next day, strain the liquid and as much sugar as possible into a small saucepan. Replace the fruit in the container.

Place the saucepan over medium-low heat and bring to a boil. Lower the heat and simmer until the syrup is reduced by half, about 20 minutes. Be careful to avoid caramelizing the syrup.

Pour the syrup over the fruit, and let sit in the refrigerator for at least 12 hours or overnight.

On day two, repeat the straining and cooking process. Once again, pour the cooked syrup over the fruit, and return the mixture to the refrigerator for at least 12 hours or overnight.

On the third day, repeat the straining and cooking process. Transfer the fruit and syrup to a blender.

Add the white wine and mustard powder. Blend until smooth, about 2 minutes.

Transfer to an airtight container and let cool. Keep refrigerated. Let sit for 1 day before serving to properly infuse the flavors. Serve at room temperature.

SEASONALITY

1. **Bloomsdale with Rosé Rhubarb (p. 112)**
2. **Carré du Berry with Rosemary Rhubarb Jelly (p. 113)**
3. **Barbablu with Pink-Pepper Pickled Rhubarb (p. 114)**

The seasonality of the produce we use in our accompaniments and the seasonality of cheese are two different subjects. Let's start with accompaniments.

Living in North America in the twenty-first century, many of us have lost touch with the seasonality of our food. We can go to the local grocery store and get peaches, tomatoes, and corn all year round. But the reality is that fruits and vegetables grow only when they are in season. That means sometimes what we eat has been shipped from far away, wherever in the world it's the right season for what we're buying.

Many of the recipes in this book are throwbacks to the days when we couldn't get whatever we wanted at the grocery store. Pickling, and making jams, chutneys, and mostardas are ways of preserving food, which our ancestors had to do in order to survive the winter. When the apricots, asparagus, berries, peaches, figs, and so on were ripe, people would can like mad so none went to waste.

The reason we eat locally grown food today isn't just for fun. Local produce from small farms is generally better tasting and more nutritious than produce from factory farms that has traveled hundreds or thousands of miles to get to your plate. Small farms are likely growing beautiful and delicious fruits and vegetables of heirloom varieties, not those that have been bred to ripen on a truck, look bright and pretty on the shelf, and taste like cardboard. If you buy fresh, local produce and preserve it, you can enjoy better food throughout the year.

Cheese can be affected by the seasons in different ways. First of all, we have to remember that cheese comes from milk, and milk comes from dairy animals. The flavors of the milk, and therefore of the cheese, are affected by what the animals eat. As a general rule in this book we talk about high-quality cheeses made from milk that comes from smaller farms where the animals are treated well. That means in the spring and summer, they are out in the pasture grazing on grasses, herbs, and flowers. The flora is determined by season and weather, but also by region (page 126). It's all intertwined.

Come fall, the animals are moved inside to live on grain, hay, or silage for the winter. The change in diet also changes the flavors of the milk, as well as other properties like fat content. A cheese made from winter milk is going to be different from one made from spring or summer milk. In some cases the differences are subtle, and maybe only professionals will be able to notice them. But in some cases the different seasons result in entirely different cheeses.

In this book we discuss several such cheeses. Winnimere (page 67), from Jasper Hill Farm in Greensboro, Vermont, is an homage to Vacherin Mont d'Or from the Jura Mountains of France. Following the same tradition, it is made only in winter when the cows are living on hay. They use the milk from spring and summer for other cheeses. Rogue River Blue (page 139), from Rogue Creamery in Central Point, Oregon, is made from spring and summer milk and is available only in the fall. (It usually sells out by early winter.)

In other cases, cheese makers choose to make certain cheeses only at certain times of the year. Some change their recipes to compensate for seasonal changes in the milk. Vermont Shepherd makes Verano from sheep's milk in the summer and Invierno from a blend of cow's and sheep's milks in the winter.

These cheeses take us back, in a way, to an era before international shipping made local seasons less of an issue on the plate. Like the summer fruits of our grandparents' childhoods, they are delicious foods that we get to enjoy for only a short time.

We believe that you should eat as much of a thing as you can while it is in season, even to the point of getting tired of it, then go without until it comes around again. In fact, we eat so much fresh local rhubarb, so many heirloom tomatoes, and so much Rogue River Blue when they are in season that by the time they are out of season we are almost relieved. Then, the next year, we start craving them again as the season draws near.

ROSÉ RHUBARB

BLOOMSDALE, BAETJE FARMS, MISSOURI
PASTEURIZED GOAT'S MILK

This is one of our favorite accompaniments with one of our favorite cheeses made by one of our favorite cheese makers. Both the Bloomsdale and the rhubarb are bright, acidic, and tangy, a great way to wake up your palate at the beginning of a platter. As much as we love Bloomsdale, it's not available everywhere. You can pair this rosé rhubarb with just about any chèvre, but look for Valençay, the ash-covered French pyramid Bloomsdale is based on.

YIELD: 2 CUPS
PREP TIME: 10 MINUTES
COOK TIME: 15 MINUTES

1 pound rhubarb

½ vanilla bean

2 cups dry rosé wine

3 tablespoons granulated sugar

1 teaspoon whole fennel seeds

Pinch of salt

Trim the tops and bottoms off the rhubarb stalks. Discard the trimmings. Cut the rhubarb into ¼-inch pieces. Set aside.

Cut the vanilla bean in half lengthwise with the tip of a paring knife. Reserve half the bean for another use. Scrape out the seeds using the tip of the knife, dragging from one end of the bean to the other.

In a medium saucepan, combine the vanilla seeds and bean, wine, sugar, fennel seeds, and salt.

Bring the liquid to a boil. Continue to boil over medium heat for 5 minutes. Turn off the heat and add the rhubarb. Let cool for 20 minutes.

Transfer to an airtight container. Keep refrigerated.

Strain before serving, or serve in a bowl with the wine.

Chef's note: Make ahead. It will keep for up to 2 weeks.

Other cheeses to serve with this accompaniment: Burrata, Selles-sur-Cher, or a young mild cheese.

Creative suggestion: Try some of the rhubarb and syrup in a glass of Champagne, Cava, or Prosecco.

ROSEMARY RHUBARB JELLY

CARRÉ DU BERRY, FROMAGERIE JACQUIN, FRANCE
PASTEURIZED GOAT'S MILK

This light, airy fresh chèvre is covered in peppercorns and herbs, so savory is taken care of. We have introduced sweet in the form of a delicate rhubarb jelly, with a touch of rosemary to tie all the elements together. It's hard to imagine a bloomy or fresh cheese that wouldn't be delicious paired with this jelly, but it is especially good with anything covered in herbs, such as brin d'amour (also known as fleur du maquis).

YIELD: 2 CUPS
PREP TIME: 10 MINUTES
COOK TIME: 15 MINUTES

8 ounces rhubarb

1½ cups granulated sugar

3 tablespoons white wine vinegar

1½ tablespoons fresh rosemary leaves, removed from the stem

3 sheets gelatin

Chef's note: Make ahead. It will keep for up to 2 weeks.

Other cheeses to serve with this accompaniment: Chèvre, Monte Enebro, or farmer's cheese.

Creative suggestion: This jelly would be elegant served on sweet toast with butter at brunch.

Have ready a heat-proof bowl with a fine-mesh strainer set in it.

Trim the tops and bottoms from the rhubarb stalks and discard the trimmings. Cut the rhubarb into 1-inch pieces.

Combine the rhubarb, 1⅓ cups water, sugar, vinegar, and rosemary in a medium saucepan and bring to a boil. Once the rhubarb is boiling, turn down the heat and simmer for 10 minutes, or until the rhubarb is soft and falls apart.

Meanwhile, place 2 cups ice in a small mixing bowl. Add cold water until the ice floats. Add the gelatin sheets. Set aside for at least 5 minutes.

Once the rhubarb is soft, turn off the heat and pour the mixture through the strainer. Press on the solids to extract as much liquid as possible. Discard the rhubarb pulp.

Remove the gelatin from the ice water. Set it on a paper towel, and lightly pat it dry to remove excess water.

Add the gelatin to the rhubarb liquid. Stir well.

Let cool, and transfer to an airtight container. Refrigerate for at least 6 hours or until set.

PINK-PEPPER PICKLED RHUBARB

BARBABLU, ITALY :: PASTEURIZED GOAT'S MILK

We like to consider Barbablu the smaller goat's-milk version of the famous, decadent monster Gorgonzola cremificato. At its peak, Barbablu can be beautifully scooped out of its soft, sticky rind and spread right on a warm piece of toast. The pickled rhubarb plays off the sweet and tart flavors of the goat's milk while also offering a crunchy texture to contrast the velvety cheese.

YIELD: 4 CUPS
PREP TIME: 10 MINUTES
COOK TIME: 10 MINUTES
TOTAL TIME: 2 DAYS

1¼ pound rhubarb

½ cup plus 2 tablespoons granulated sugar

⅓ cup tarragon vinegar

⅓ cup rice vinegar

1 bay leaf

2 teaspoons whole pink peppercorns

Pinch of salt

Trim the tops and bottoms off the rhubarb stalks. Discard the trimmings. Cut the rhubarb into ¼-inch pieces, and place in a 32-ounce glass pickling jar. Set aside.

In a medium saucepan, combine ¾ cup of water and the remaining ingredients (except the rhubarb).

Bring the liquid to a boil, stirring occasionally. Remove from the heat and let cool for 10 minutes.

Pour the pickling liquid over the rhubarb until it covers the rhubarb completely. Immediately put the lid on the jar while the liquid is still warm.

Place in the refrigerator and keep for 2 days before serving to properly infuse the flavors.

Serve at room temperature.

Chef's notes: If you are unable to find tarragon vinegar, use white wine vinegar and add 2 tablespoons of chopped fresh tarragon to the rhubarb.

Make ahead. It will keep for up to 1 month.

Other cheeses to serve with this accompaniment: Young goat cheese, Verde Capra, or a mild, sweet blue.

Creative suggestion: Try this sweet and tart pickle as an accompaniment with pâté.

1. Rollingstone Chèvre with Baba Ghanoush (p. 120)
2. Ibores with Sweet and Sour Lotus Root (p. 123)
3. Cayuga Blue with Honeycomb (p. 124)

Manufactured cheese is made to be consistently the same regardless of where or when it is purchased. These industrial cheeses are most likely to come from the milk of cows living in feedlots who eat the same thing, probably corn, year round. The cheeses are shelf-stable, designed to last as long as possible without changing.

Real cheese, on the other hand, is a living thing. It is full of all sorts of microflora such as bacteria, yeasts, and molds. These microbes multiply and grow, changing the cheese as it ages. A young Époisses (page 156) may be slightly pliant in texture, although the same cheese a few weeks later will have a runny liquid in the center. A four-month-old Cheddar will be much milder and softer than the same wheel at two years old. Generally, flavors get more intense and concentrated in older cheeses as the microorganisms multiply and the moisture evaporates. But some cheeses are meant to be eaten young, and they get kind of yucky when past their prime. A twelve-month Piave is great. A twelve-month Camembert, not so much.

Finding exactly the right accompaniment for a cheese can be challenging because it's a moving target. Because of seasonality cheese can taste different from wheel to wheel or batch to batch. Even a single wheel can be different from day to day, week to week, month to month, or year to year, because as it ages it changes.

That leads us to our big caveat. All the pairings that we suggest in this book are great, but we don't promise that they are perfect all the time. We advise you to approach these suggestions with an open mind, and we strongly encourage you to experiment on your own. If a pairing doesn't work, think about why. Test accompaniments with cheeses beyond what we suggest here. Work with your cheesemonger to find the best alternatives. Find cheeses you like, and imagine what flavors would complement or contrast with them. Give your palate a chance to get into shape by tasting lots of foods, and get creative with your cheese plates.

We can't tell you which exact cheeses and pairings to put on your plate because things change too much when they are living organisms. Instead, we are arming you with the tools and knowledge you need to make choices on your own. Go ahead. We trust you.

BABA GHANOUSH

CHÈVRE, ROLLINGSTONE, IDAHO :: PASTEURIZED GOAT'S MILK

There is no shortage of excellent chèvre in North America, but Rollingstone's is the creamiest we've ever tasted, with the texture of a light, fluffy goat's-milk cloud. The smooth roasted eggplant balances and applauds the gamy forwardness of the cheese. Rollingstone is not widely available, but that's not a problem because you can pair this baba ghanoush with any good, fresh chèvre.

YIELD: 2 CUPS
PREP TIME: 5 MINUTES
COOK TIME: 1½ HOURS PLUS 50 MINUTES

1 head garlic

5 tablespoons extra-virgin olive oil, divided

1 large eggplant, about 2 pounds

2 tablespoons fresh parsley

¼ cup tahini

1½ teaspoons salt

1 teaspoon freshly grated lemon zest

Preheat the oven to 300°F.

Cut a ¼-inch slice off the top of the garlic bulb to expose the tops of the cloves. Place the garlic cut-side down on a sheet of aluminum foil. Fold the edges of the foil upward around the garlic to create a cup. Add 3 tablespoons of olive oil. Seal the foil.

Set the foil-wrapped garlic in a glass or metal baking dish, and bake for 1 to 1½ hours. The garlic should be golden-brown and tender. Remove from the oven and let cool.

Squeeze the garlic bulb or peel back the skin to release the roasted garlic cloves. If you're not using the garlic right away, store it in an airtight container. Keep refrigerated.

Preheat the oven to 375°F.

Line a baking sheet with parchment paper. Place the eggplant on the baking sheet and rub it with 2 tablespoons olive oil until coated. Pierce a few times with a paring knife.

Bake for 30 to 40 minutes. The skin should be slightly brown and the flesh very tender, almost mushy. Remove from the oven and let cool.

Cut open the eggplant and remove all the flesh from the skin. Discard the skin. Place the eggplant in a medium mixing bowl.

Roughly chop the parsley.

Add the parsley, 5 cloves of the roasted garlic, and the remaining ingredients to the eggplant. Whisk the mixture until combined and smooth, about 1 minute.

Store in an airtight container. Keep refrigerated. Serve at room temperature.

Chef's note: Make ahead. It will keep for up to 5 days.

Other cheeses to serve with this accompaniment: Cottage cheese, Brie, Camembert, or a mild bloomy-rind cheese.

Creative suggestion: Serve with flatbread or chips for a light snack.

Cheese as a Living Thing

SWEET AND SOUR LOTUS ROOT

IBORES, SPAIN :: RAW GOAT'S MILK

You may have to seek out an Asian grocery store for the lotus root, but it's worth the effort. Visually, this dish is a stunner. The taste of the sweet and sour sauce is reminiscent of teriyaki. Lotus root retains a wonderful crunch after it is cooked, much like a water chestnut. The Ibores, which is rubbed in paprika, has a wonderful, swift, kung fu kick of acidity. You will feel this one on your tongue!

YIELD: 2 CUPS
PREP TIME: 10 MINUTES
COOK TIME: 20 MINUTES

¼ cup lime juice

¼ cup ketchup

3 ounces light brown sugar

2 tablespoons soy sauce

¼ cup rice vinegar

¼ cup fish sauce

¼ teaspoon red chili flakes

1½ tablespoons black sesame seeds

2 garlic cloves, minced

1 tablespoon sesame oil

1 tablespoon extra-virgin olive oil

1 pound prepared lotus root (see Chef's Notes; or use fresh lotus root, peeled and sliced into ⅛-inch-thick rounds)

In a medium mixing bowl, stir together the lime juice, ketchup, brown sugar, soy sauce, vinegar, fish sauce, chili flakes, sesame seeds, and garlic until combined. Set aside.

Drain the prepared lotus root.

In a large saucepan, heat the sesame and olive oils over medium-high heat for 1 minute. Add the lotus root. Cook for 3 minutes. Toss the lotus root, and continue to cook for another 3 minutes.

Add the sauce to the lotus root in the pan, and toss to cover the lotus root with the sauce.

Reduce the heat to medium-low and cover the pan. Continue to cook until the sauce glazes the root and is thickened, about 12 to 15 minutes. Remove from the heat and let cool.

Store in an airtight container. Keep refrigerated. Serve at room temperature.

Chef's notes: Prepared lotus root can be found in the refrigerated produce aisle of most Asian grocery stores. It has been peeled and cut into thin rounds and is usually packed in water in a plastic bag.

Make ahead. It will keep for up to 1 week.

Other cheeses to serve with this accompaniment: Shelburne Farms Smoked Cheddar, feta, or Capriole Old Kentucky Tomme.

Creative suggestion: Serve these crunchy rounds on top of sautéed greens with garlic.

HONEYCOMB

CAYUGA BLUE, LIVELY RUN GOAT DAIRY, NEW YORK :: RAW GOAT'S MILK

Clean and sharp, this cheese from the Finger Lakes region of New York is turned into a dessert by being paired with brittle, sweet honeycomb. The slight bitterness of the cooked honey complements many cheeses, especially Cheddar or Gouda. You can make it at the last minute and have it on hand for days of snacking.

YIELD: 3 QUARTS
PREP TIME: 5 MINUTES
COOK TIME: 20 MINUTES

1 cup granulated sugar

¼ cup light corn syrup

¼ cup wildflower or clover honey

1 tablespoon baking soda

½ teaspoon salt

Chef's note: Make ahead. It will keep for up to 2 months with no humidity.

Other cheeses to serve with this accompaniment: A drier sweet cheese like Gouda or aged Cheddar, or a strong blue.

Creative suggestion: Chop the honeycomb into small pieces and layer it between soft peanut butter cookies with a smear of peanut butter for a dessert sandwich with a crunchy bite!

Line a baking sheet with a nonstick baking liner.

Combine the sugar, corn syrup, and honey in a small saucepan over medium heat. Stir the mixture with a heat-resistant spatula as it melts and comes to a boil. Remove the spatula once the mixture is at a boil.

Continue to cook over medium heat until the sugar changes color from a light amber to a medium amber, about 15 minutes. You do not want to overcook the caramel, which will result in a bitter taste.

Remove the caramel from the heat, and stir in the baking soda and salt. The blend will instantly bubble up. Quickly but gently, continue to stir the caramel until all the baking soda is dissolved. Immediately pour the honeycomb onto the baking sheet.

Gently smooth out the honeycomb to an even layer. Be careful not to deflate it too much. Let it cool to room temperature. To serve, cut the honeycomb in half to expose the "hive" of bubbles inside.

Store in an airtight container, broken into large pieces. Keep at room temperature, away from humidity or light.

REGIONALITY

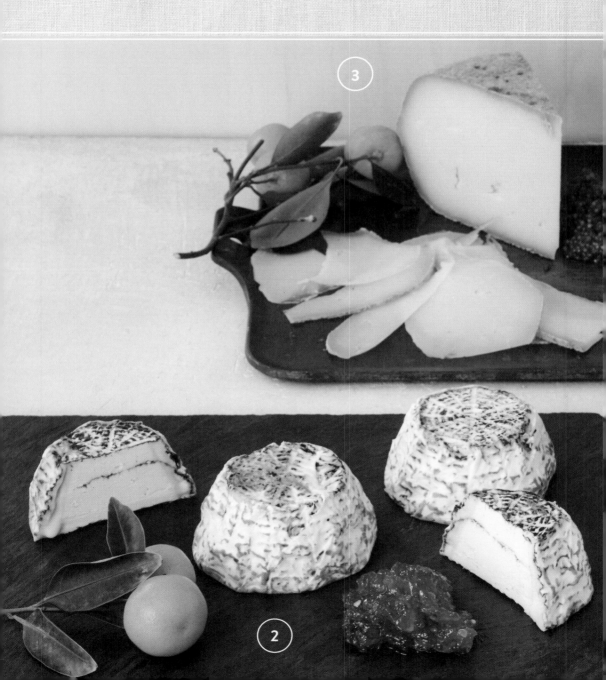

1. Coupole with Spiced Carrot Chutney (p. 131)
2. Thin Red Line with Sweet and Spicy Red Pepper Jelly (p. 133)
3. Pawlet with Bacon Molasses Mustard (p. 134)
4. Mad River Blue with Lemon Roasted Asparagus (p. 136)

If you know a little about wine, you know that where a wine comes from, often referred to as terroir, makes a huge difference in how it tastes. Grapes come from the ground, and what that ground is made up of affects the flavor of the grape, and the wine that comes from the grape, immensely. The weather in a particular region determines which grapes are planted there, and the weather in a given year affects how the grapes, and therefore the wine, turn out.

Cheese is no different. Dairy animals eat the grasses, herbs, and flowers that come from the ground where they live, and those all affect how the milk and subsequent cheese will taste. Weather has an effect, too. In California, the animals live outside and graze for more of the year than the animals in Vermont or Switzerland do. In regions with harsh winters, animals live though the winter on hay, silage, grain, or alfalfa, causing some cheeses to taste different depending on when in the year they were made. That's seasonality (page 108), but it's also regionality.

Environment affects the end result, too. When a French affineur places a new cheese in the aging cave, molds settle on the cheese, and as they grow and age they create the rind and impart flavors to the cheese. The same things happen in North Carolina and Oregon, but the molds in those environments are different, so they have a different effect on the resulting cheese. Different nutrients and flavors in the diets of the animals, different bacteria in the milks, and different molds and yeasts in the environment all lead to subtle, or not so subtle, differences in the cheeses.

Regional differences can be concealed. When a milk is pasteurized, most of the good bacteria are killed, along with any potentially dangerous ones. They are then replaced with commercial cultures. The commercial bacteria grow and multiply and create all kinds of flavors and aromas in the cheeses, but they aren't unique to their locality. Cheese makers have many options; they choose the commercially available cultures that bring about the flavors and other characteristics they want. The result is that a cheese from

California and a cheese from Virginia may be made with the same cultures. Regionality foiled!

In the United States, in the twenty-first century, we have embraced the fact that most of us have access to hundreds of cheeses from all around the world. We can procure cheeses from specialty food stores, cheese shops, Whole Foods, Central Market, co-ops, and other cheese sellers all over the country. And for those not lucky enough to live near a good source of international cheese, we have the Internet and overnight delivery. This is both a blessing and a curse because, to a large extent, we have lost touch with regionality.

There was a time when regionality was everyone's reality out of necessity. You ate what came from the farms around you because that was what was available. You found lots of Gouda in Holland, Emmentaler in Switzerland, Cheddar in the UK, and so on. Regionality in most of what we call the Old World remains important, in spite of the convenience of international food-distribution systems, because farmers choose to maintain their traditions. With cheeses, in many cases, laws and regulations require it. So you still find fresh and bloomy-rind goat's-milk cheeses from the Loire Valley and blue sheep's-milk cheeses from Roquefort in France, Robiola from Piedmont in Northern Italy, and Idiazabal from the Basque region of Spain. In the United States, by contrast, we don't have much of a cheese tradition, so we are not bound to regional styles as they are in the Old World. There is great mozzarella being made in Dallas, Texas, and Brooklyn, New York. Fresh chèvre is everywhere. There are dairies that make Swiss-style Emmentaler, British-style Cheddar, French-style Brie, and Greek-style feta, along with their own "American originals." In Europe, you can guess where a cheese is from based on how it looks. Not so in the United States.

Regardless of tradition, it's good to eat foods that are local because getting them from farm to table often leaves a smaller carbon footprint than procuring foods from far away. Furthermore, by buying local you support your local farmers, which is great, and the foods are fresher, tastier, and more nutritious. If you are lucky enough to live in New England, in Wisconsin, or on the West Coast, you have an abundance of cheese choices. But define local as best you can. In San Francisco you have plenty within a hundred miles. In other places, you may have to define local as five hundred miles in order to have enough to choose from. But no matter where you live, there are at least a few good, local cheese makers.

We think it's fun to mix up the regions on a cheese plate so that your guests can have the opportunity to experience the differences, but occasionally we like to focus on a particular region. There are so many different styles of cheeses from places such as Wisconsin or the Pacific Northwest—not to mention most of Europe—that it's easy to create a regional cheese plate of great variety, like we have done here with a simple all-Vermont plate (page 126).

SPICED CARROT CHUTNEY

COUPOLE, VERMONT CREAMERY, VERMONT
PASTEURIZED GOAT'S MILK

Beneath the hypnotizing brainy-looking rind of this French-inspired, aged goat cheese is a dense and fudgy paste. "Coupole-ing" it with this perky chutney will energize your taste buds.

YIELD: 2 CUPS
PREP TIME: 20 MINUTES
COOK TIME: 25 MINUTES

1 pound medium carrots

1 small yellow onion

2 garlic cloves

1 ounce fresh ginger, peeled and coarsely chopped

1 cup white wine vinegar

2 tablespoons yellow mustard seeds

2 teaspoons cumin seeds

½ cup golden raisins

½ cup light brown sugar

1 teaspoon salt

Peel the carrots and trim off the tops and bottoms. Grate the carrots on the largest hole of a box grater. Yield will be about 3 cups. Set aside.

Peel the onion. Grate it on the largest hole of a box grater. Set aside.

Purée the garlic, ginger, and vinegar in a blender, on high, for 2 minutes or until smooth.

Combine all ingredients in a medium saucepan. Bring to a boil over medium heat. Cook, stirring occasionally, over medium heat for about 15 minutes, or until most of the liquid is reduced.

Remove the chutney from the heat and let it cool to room temperature.

Store in an airtight container. Keep refrigerated. Serve at room temperature.

Chef's notes: Asian markets usually carry premade puréed garlic and ginger in jars. Feel free to make your own from fresh ingredients. I promise you won't be disappointed in the bright flavor!

Make ahead. It will keep for up to 1 week.

Other cheeses to serve with this accompaniment: Feta, farmer's cheese, or another salty pressed cheese.

Creative suggestion: Add half a small head of green cabbage, sliced, and double the spices for a different version of slaw.

SWEET AND SPICY RED PEPPER JELLY

THIN RED LINE, LAZY LADY FARM, VERMONT
PASTEURIZED GOAT'S MILK

This delicate little ash-covered beauty is named for the line of smoked paprika that runs through its pure white center. We love it, not only for its visual impact on the plate, but also for its tangy, zesty flavor. The spicy/sweet contrast of the red pepper jelly plays wonderfully against the subtle smoky aromas in the cheese while adding a splash of color to your plate. You can try the jelly with any soft cheese spread on bread or toast, but we like this pairing undiluted by bread, too (see page 96).

YIELD: 2 CUPS

PREP TIME: 10 MINUTES

COOK TIME: 30 MINUTES PLUS 8 HOURS

1 red bell pepper, about 6 ounces

1½ cups granulated sugar

2 tablespoons dry pectin

½ cup white wine vinegar

½ teaspoon red chili flakes

Set aside a clean, dry 16-ounce glass pickling jar.

Remove the stem and seeds from the pepper and discard. Cut the pepper into 1-inch pieces. Purée the pepper in a blender or food processor about 1 minute, or until it has a consistent texture.

Meanwhile, in a small mixing bowl, combine the sugar and pectin. Mix well. Set aside.

Combine the red pepper, vinegar, and chili flakes in a medium saucepan and bring to a boil over medium heat. Reduce to a simmer.

Vigorously whisk in the sugar mixture in a slow steady stream. Return to a boil. Insert a thermometer. Continue to boil over medium heat until the liquid reaches 220°F, about 20 minutes.

Once the temperature is reached, turn off the heat. Skim off any light-colored foam using a spoon or ladle.

Transfer the jelly to the jar and refrigerate for at least 8 hours, or until firm.

Keep refrigerated. Serve at room temperature.

Chef's Note: Make ahead. It will keep for up to 1 month.

Other cheeses to serve with this accompaniment: Humboldt Fog, chèvre, or cream cheese.

Creative suggestion: Try using different-colored peppers, such as yellow, orange, or green.

BACON MOLASSES MUSTARD

PAWLET, CONSIDER BARDWELL FARM, VERMONT :: RAW COW'S MILK

We know we had you at bacon, but this pairing is so much more. Pawlet, a natural-rind cow's-milk cheese, is named after the town in which it is made. It is pliable and creamy, the perfect foundation for the sharp, acidic, bright flavors of the mustard. Bacon just makes everything better. If you are serving your Pawlet on slate, it just may have come from the same place as the cheese! The town of Pawlet is in an area known as Slate Valley.

YIELD: 2 CUPS
PREP TIME: 20 MINUTES
COOK TIME: 20 MINUTES
TOTAL TIME: 2 DAYS

1 cup yellow mustard seeds

1 cup white wine vinegar

¼ cup dry white wine (e.g., pinot grigio)

2 tablespoons light brown sugar

4 ounces smoked bacon

1 tablespoon bacon fat, reserved from cooking bacon

1 teaspoon ground cinnamon

¼ cup plus 1 tablespoon molasses

Pinch of salt

Combine the mustard seeds, vinegar, wine, and brown sugar in a 32-ounce pickling jar, or in a metal or plastic container. Let the mustard seeds soak, covered, at room temperature for at least 12 hours or overnight.

Preheat the oven to 350°F.

Line a baking sheet with parchment paper. Lay the bacon in a single layer on the baking sheet. Bake until crispy, about 12 to 15 minutes.

Remove the bacon from the oven. Reserve 1 tablespoon of bacon fat. Set aside. Once the bacon is cool, chop into small pieces.

Add bacon, bacon fat, cinnamon, molasses, and salt to the soaked mustard seeds.

Using a hand blender, blend the mustard until it starts to thicken and hold its shape. Don't blend too long; you want to avoid breaking apart the seeds and turning the mixture into a purée. (But even if you blend a little too long, it will still taste good!) If you are using a stand blender or food processor, pulse the mustard a few times to reach the desired consistency.

Spoon the mustard into an airtight container. Store in the refrigerator for at least 1 day before serving to infuse the flavors.

Chef's note: Make ahead. It will keep for up to 3 weeks in the fridge.

Other cheeses to serve with this accompaniment: Mimolette, Point Reyes Toma, or an Alpine cheese like Gruyère or Comté.

Creative suggestion: Don't worry about leftovers because you are going to want to put this mustard on your sandwiches, burgers, and hot dogs!

LEMON ROASTED ASPARAGUS

MAD RIVER BLUE, VON TRAPP FARMSTEAD, VERMONT
RAW COW'S MILK

Mad River Blue is buttery and complex, showcasing an approachable mild blue mold. Here, we've gone in the other direction, with savory, salty asparagus. In this pairing, the sweet organic milk balances the strong, vegetal notes of the asparagus.

YIELD: 2 CUPS
PREP TIME: 10 MINUTES
COOK TIME: 20 MINUTES

1 pound asparagus

3 tablespoons extra-virgin olive oil

1 teaspoon salt

1 tablespoon unsalted butter

Grated zest from 1 medium lemon

Preheat the oven to 400°F.

Line a baking sheet with parchment paper. Set aside.

Cut the bottom 2 inches off the asparagus spears to remove the tough, fibrous stems. Discard the trimmings. Cut the asparagus into ⅛-inch-thick pieces.

Combine the asparagus, oil, and salt in a medium mixing bowl. Toss well to coat.

Spread the asparagus on the baking sheet in an even layer. Bake for 20 minutes, or until tender and slightly charred.

Remove the asparagus from the oven and place on a heat-proof surface. Add the butter and lemon zest while the asparagus is still hot, and toss until coated.

Let cool to room temperature. Store in an airtight container. Keep refrigerated. Serve at room temperature.

Chef's note: Make ahead. It will keep for up to 3 days.

Other cheeses to serve with this accompaniment: Arpea, Raclette, or an aged English Cheddar.

Creative suggestion: Toss with fresh chopped tomato and summer squash for a colorful summer salad.

BEVERAGES

1. Spoonwood Cabin Feta with Carrot Cumin Purée (p. 145)
2. Crémeux des Augustins with Mushroom Duxelles (p. 150)
3. Red Hawk with Blood Orange Fennel Chip (p. 146)
4. Barely Buzzed with Anise Meringue (p. 148)
5. Rogue River Blue with Toasted Walnut Pesto (p. 150)

You can go in one of two directions when pairing beverages with cheese plates: intellectual or emotional. The intellectual style involves choosing one beverage for each cheese, as we have done on page 138, where we have paired a manzanilla sherry with feta from Spoonwood Cabin in Vermont, a Prosecco with Crémeux des Augustins, a pinot noir with Red Hawk from Cowgirl Creamery in Sonoma, an espresso stout with Barely Buzzed from Beehive Cheese in Utah, and a sake with Rogue River Blue from Rogue Creamery in Oregon.

When you pair like this, each bite and each sip is an experiment, an education in taste combinations. Each pairing is a topic for you and your guests to study. You taste a cheese by itself, then sip the beverage. You then taste the cheese with its condiment and consider the pairing. You nod knowingly at your tasting companions, then sip the beverage again and see how the drink changes the whole combination. You take notes.

For the right group of people at the right time, this can be a great experience. It can be fun—intellectual, dorky, geeky, nerdy, left-brain fun. For a lot of people, and in a lot of situations, however, this intellectual pairing can be too much work, and it can seem kind of obnoxious or intimidating. That's why, for most people, most of the time, it makes more sense to keep it simple—or emotional.

The emotional style is to pick a beverage that you like and that, in a broad sense, goes well with cheese. With a nice bottle of pinot noir or a good microbrewed beer, you can relax and enjoy the cheese plate and the beverage without being distracted by either. You can create the cheese plate and then decide what to drink with it, but we recommend choosing the beverage first—say, a bottle of wine—and then creating a plate that will pair well with it. It also works well for everyone to choose a beverage of his or her own.

Most of the time when we sit down at the table we are there to commune with other human beings. That means we want to tell stories and make each other laugh and feel and connect. If we want to think, we want to think about our friends, not the chemical makeup of our food and its effects on our palates. We want to feed our souls while we fill our bellies. The cheese and the wine do both, but we want to leave room for the conversation.

For this reason, we do not normally serve flights of wine or beverage pairings at Casellula. We will do so upon request, but we are rarely asked. Most white wines, sparkling wines, beers, sakes, sherries, ports, meads, and Madeiras are very good with a broad range of cheeses. Many red wines are, too. So relax, and choose to drink something you like. Chances are it's not going to screw up the cheese plate, and it will make you happy.

What makes us the happiest to drink with our cheese plate is bubbles. When you take a bite of cheese, your mouth becomes coated with protein and fat molecules. If you then take a sip of Champagne, Prosecco, Cava, or a good craft beer, the acid and the bubbles clean the fat right off your tongue and refresh your palate. That makes you want to have another bite of cheese, which makes you want to take a sip of your drink, and back and forth you go, with fat, protein, bubbles, and acid playing an exciting mixed-doubles tennis match on your tongue.

This is not to say that we don't like other beverages with our cheese plates. Really, we are most likely to drink whatever we are having with our meal with our cheese plates, and in most cases that means wine or beer. Most white wines serve a broad range of cheeses very well. The wine has acid and the cheese has fat, and they are going to play around together on your palate. We would shy away from heavy, oaky chardonnays, but otherwise drink what you like. (Remember, there are no rules, so drink all the chardonnay you want if that's your thing.)

If you want to broaden your white wine horizons a little, try a gewürz-traminer (spicy, sometimes a little sweet), grüner veltliner (crisp like fresh apples), or albariño (a versatile Spanish wine that goes with everything). Rieslings, which range from the cloyingly sweet to the elegantly dry, can be great with cheese plates. The different levels of sweetness work with differ-ent cheeses in different ways and for different palates. We like a midlevel sweetness, but choose the sweetness level you like and dive in.

When drinking reds with a range of cheeses, we lean toward the light bodied, and that usually points to pinot noir. The best of them, from Bur-gundy, the Willamette Valley, New Zealand, Austria, and Italy, are light in body but full of flavor and high in acid—and therefore perfect with many, many cheeses. But pinots aren't the only light red wines. Gamay, which is the grape in Beaujolais, can be beautiful. We're not talking about Beaujolais Nouveau, the unaged homage to quick cash flow that emerges from France every November. We are talking about Beaujolais Cru, which are wines that can be as complex and delicious as any. We also like grignolino, gaglioppo, barbera, dolcetto, and mencía with our cheese plates. If you like full-bodied red wines such as cabernet sauvignon, zinfandel, or malbec, we suggest you lean toward hard, aged cheeses that have the strength to stand up to the alcohol in those wines.

Craft beers come in all styles, so there is something for every kind of cheese. You can aim to pair specific flavors, drinking fruity beers with fruity cheeses and nutty beers with nutty cheeses and so on. Or you can think more broadly and drink a light lager or ale with softer, more delicate cheeses and a heavier stout or porter with aged cheeses. There will be no end to the experimenting, though, as there are more beers and cheeses available than you will ever get to!

Plenty of professionals out there will tell you that *this* beverage goes with *this* cheese. They are very often right about a particular pairing, and we get as excited about those moments as anyone else. But the truth is that many different beverage pairings work for each cheese and for each cheese platter, and what is right depends on the person doing the tasting. So you do you. Think in broad strokes to find one beverage that complements a variety of cheeses, which is how you will be eating and drinking most of the time. Think creatively when you are pairing more specifically. The only rule that matters is: if you like it, it's good!

CARROT CUMIN PURÉE

FETA, SPOONWOOD CABIN, VERMONT :: RAW COW'S MILK

Enjoy the Spoonwood Cabin feta, or any of their other wonderful cheeses, when you are in southern Vermont or New York City, but don't expect to find them all over the country. Instead, choose whatever feta is local to you. The carrot cumin purée benefits from the saltiness of the cheese, and the cheese from the sweetness and spiciness of the purée.

YIELD: 2 CUPS
PREP TIME: 15 MINUTES
COOK TIME: 25 MINUTES

1 pound medium carrots

2 medium shallots

3 tablespoons unsalted butter

2 garlic cloves, finely chopped

½ cup orange juice

1 teaspoon ground cumin

2½ teaspoons salt

Peel the carrots and trim the tops and bottoms, discarding the scraps. Slice the carrots into ¼-inch rounds.

Peel the shallots and slice them into ⅛-inch rounds.

In a medium saucepan, heat the butter for 2 minutes over medium heat. Add the carrots, shallots, and garlic. Cook for 5 minutes, stirring once.

Add the orange juice, cumin, and salt. Toss to combine evenly. Cover. Continue to cook on medium-low heat, stirring occasionally, for 15 minutes or until the carrots are soft and all the juice is absorbed.

Transfer the carrots to a blender. Add ½ cup of water. Purée on high for 2 minutes or until smooth. Scrape down the sides to blend.

Store in an airtight container. Keep refrigerated. Serve at room temperature.

Chef's notes: If you do not have a blender, a food processor is recommended.

Make ahead. It will keep for up to 5 days.

Other cheeses to serve with this accompaniment: Ibores, Havarti, or a fresh, mild cheese.

Creative suggestion: Use this as a savory spread on sandwiches.

BLOOD ORANGE FENNEL CHIP

RED HAWK, COWGIRL CREAMERY, CALIFORNIA :: PASTEURIZED COW'S MILK

In terms of its visual appeal, this is one of our favorite accompaniments. The crisp crunch of the chip serves the role of a cracker, and the taste is bitter and tart with an undercurrent of sweetness and a lovely aromatic note from the fennel. The Red Hawk, a washed-rind version of Cowgirl's Mt. Tam, is a triple-crème ball of velvety deliciousness with just enough stink to play nice with the aromatics from the fennel. The chip is great in combination with other accompaniments such as coffee cajeta or blackberry honey.

YIELD: ABOUT 30 CHIPS
PREP TIME: 20 MINUTES
COOK TIME: 1 TO 2 HOURS

2 blood oranges

1 cup granulated sugar

¼ cup whole fennel seeds

Preheat the oven to 200°F. Line a baking sheet with parchment paper.

Using a slicer or mandoline, slice the whole, unpeeled oranges crosswise as thinly as possible.

In a small saucepan, bring the sugar and 1 cup of water to a boil for 1 minute. Turn off the heat and let cool.

Dip an orange slice into the sugar syrup for 2 seconds. Remove the orange slice and let the excess syrup drip off. Repeat with all the slices.

Arrange the orange slices on the baking sheet. Do not let them overlap or they will stick to each other. Sprinkle the fennel seeds over the slices.

Bake for 1 to 2 hours. Rotate the sheet tray every 30 minutes. To see if the oranges are crisp, remove one from the sheet and place it on the counter to cool. When it's cool, try to snap it. If it bends, continue baking for another 30 minutes.

Remove the chips from the oven. While they're still warm, lift them off the baking sheet. Place them back on the baking sheet to cool.

Store in an airtight container at room temperature.

Chef's notes: If you are unable to find blood oranges, you may substitute with navel.

Make ahead. They will keep for up to 1 month with no humidity.

Other cheeses to serve with this accompaniment: San Andreas, Manchego, or a strong sheep's-milk cheese.

Creative suggestions: Use other fruits like apple, pear, or pineapple. Experiment with different seasonings.

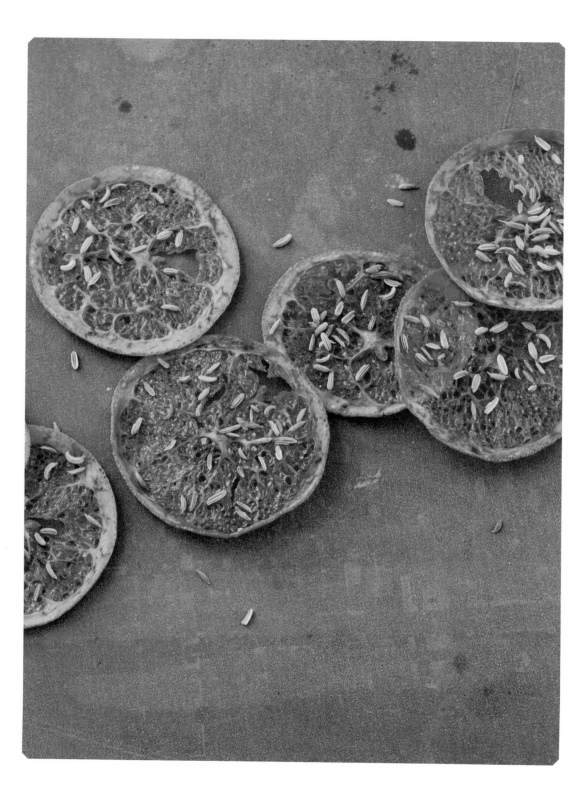

ANISE MERINGUE

BARELY BUZZED, BEEHIVE CHEESE COMPANY, UTAH
PASTEURIZED COW'S MILK

Our good friends at Beehive Cheese in Ogden, Utah, have a fun sense of irony. They are Mormons and therefore don't drink coffee or alcohol, yet they have rubbed their flagship cheese with espresso and lavender and called it Barely Buzzed. We have paired it here with a crunchy anise meringue. Anise, an herb with flavors similar to those of fennel and licorice, complements both the lavender and the espresso notes in the cheese. The crunch is a fun contrast to the fudgy texture of the cheese.

YIELD: 4 CUPS
PREP TIME: 5 MINUTES
COOK TIME: 2 HOURS

3 large egg whites

¾ cup granulated sugar

¼ teaspoon cornstarch

½ teaspoon vanilla extract

Pinch of salt

1 teaspoon ground anise seed

1 teaspoon fresh lemon zest

Preheat the oven to 200°F.

Line a baking sheet with parchment paper and set aside.

Bring a pot of shallow water to a simmer. Reduce the heat to low.

Combine the egg whites, sugar, and cornstarch in the mixing bowl of a stand mixer. Place the bowl over the simmering water (be careful not to let the bowl rest in the water). Whisk the mixture by hand until the sugar is completely melted and the mixture is slightly warm. The egg whites will be thin and a little foamy. If you rub a bit of the mixture between your fingers, it should be smooth. Remove from heat.

Return the bowl to the mixer. Beat on high for 5 minutes, or until the mixture is thick and glossy and has tripled in volume. Reduce the speed to medium and add the vanilla, salt, anise seed, and lemon zest.

Continue to mix until incorporated.

Remove the bowl from the mixer. Gently fold the meringue from the bottom of the bowl to the top to evenly distribute.

Place half the meringue in a clean, dry piping bag fitted with a small, round piping tip. Holding the tip directly above the baking sheet, pipe 1-inch buttons, kisses, or whatever shape you like. Continue with the remaining meringue.

Bake for approximately 2 hours, depending on the meringues' size, until crisp. To see if they are dry, remove one of the meringues from the oven and let cool. If it's dry, it will snap in half. Once the meringues are fully cooked, remove from the oven and let cool.

Carefully peel the meringues off the parchment and place in an airtight container. Store at room temperature.

Chef's notes: If you are baking in a convection oven with a fan, place a dot of meringue in each corner underneath the parchment paper to act as glue.

Make ahead. These will last for several months without humidity.

Other cheeses to serve with this accompaniment: La Tur, Grafton Village One Year Aged Cheddar, or a mild, sweet blue.

Creative suggestions: Serve as a petit four with espresso or amaro, or use as an ice cream topping.

MUSHROOM DUXELLES

CRÉMEUX DES AUGUSTINS, FRANCE :: PASTEURIZED COW'S MILK

Everything about this pairing is luxurious. Mushroom duxelles is a decadent blend of savory mushrooms with herbs and cream. Crémeux des Augustins is a buttery, umami-packed bloomy rind wrapped in bark. You will need a spoon for this pairing, but we think you will have a hard time putting it down!

YIELD: 2 CUPS
PREP TIME: 15 MINUTES
COOK TIME: 20 MINUTES

2 medium shallots

14 ounces shiitake mushrooms

6 ounces unsalted butter

¼ cup extra-virgin olive oil

½ cup Madeira or sherry wine

2 tablespoons parsley

1 teaspoon fresh thyme leaves, removed from the stem

¼ cup heavy cream

1½ teaspoons salt

Peel the shallots, and chop them into small pieces.

Remove the stems from the shiitake caps and discard. Place the caps flat on a cutting board. Slice into very thin strips, about ⅛ inch thick.

In a medium saucepan over medium heat, warm the butter and olive oil together, about 4 minutes.

Add the shallots and cook for 3 to 5 minutes, until they become translucent.

Add the sliced shiitake. Stir well. Cook over medium heat until the mushrooms are soft, about 8 to 10 minutes.

Add the wine, parsley, and thyme. Continue to cook over medium heat for 7 minutes, stirring occasionally. Remove from the heat and stir to cool for 2 minutes.

Add the heavy cream and salt. Stir to emulsify the cream into the butter. If the blend looks a bit separated, add a little more cream and stir to combine.

Let cool to room temperature. Store in an airtight container. Keep refrigerated. Warm slightly before serving to smooth out the sauce. Serve at room temperature.

Chef's note: Make ahead. It will keep for up to 5 days.

Other cheeses to serve with this accompaniment: Mt. Tam, Camembert, or Taleggio.

Creative suggestion: Try serving this as a creamy sauce over meatballs or polenta.

TOASTED WALNUT PESTO

ROGUE RIVER BLUE, ROGUE CREAMERY, OREGON :: RAW COW'S MILK

This is a truly special seasonal blue. Our friends at Rogue Creamery in southern Oregon have wrapped their flagship cheese in grape leaves from a neighboring vineyard that have been soaked in a local pear eau-de-vie. The texture is creamy, and the flavors are as layered and complex as it gets. Toasted walnut pesto plays nicely with the fruitiness of the liqueur, whose concentrated sweetness creates a delicious tension with the cheese's sharp blue kick.

YIELD: 2 CUPS
PREP TIME: 15 MINUTES
COOK TIME: 10 MINUTES

2½ cups walnut pieces

3 ounces pecorino

⅓ cup walnut oil

1 garlic clove

½ teaspoon salt

Preheat the oven to 325°F.

Line a baking sheet with parchment paper. Spread the walnuts on the baking sheet in a single, even layer. Toast the walnuts until golden, about 10 minutes. Remove from the oven and let cool.

Grate the pecorino on the largest hole of a box grater.

Combine the walnuts in a food processor with the pecorino, oil, garlic, and salt. Pulse the mixture about 10 to 12 times, until smooth but not puréed. You want a bit of a chunky texture.

Store the pesto in an airtight container. Keep refrigerated. Serve at room temperature.

Chef's note: Make ahead. It will keep for up to 2 weeks.

Other cheeses to serve with this accompaniment: Raschera, Reblochon, or Manchego.

Creative suggestion: Mix the pesto with a bunch of fresh basil, chopped, and some olive oil to create a simple pasta sauce.

Are you hosting a sit-down dinner party for eight friends, or are you taking the cheese course to a pot-luck for twenty? Hosting your wife's boss for dinner, or thirty women for a wedding shower? Different occasions call for different cheese presentations.

When we talk about cheese plates we generally mean one of three types: a plate that is served to an individual guest as a course in a meal; a plate that is shared in the middle of a table; or a platter to which a large number of guests can help themselves, likely before or in place of a meal. Each is right for a different occasion.

Here we've plated Bayley Hazen Blue with a chocolate graham cracker in a pairing intended for one person (opposite page). A cheese with a sweet pairing like this can be served as an alternative to dessert. Just about any single cheese with an accompaniment can be served as a small course between dinner and dessert.

For intimate occasions, like a romantic dinner for two or a small gathering of friends, a shared plate in the middle of the table, similar to what we do at Casellula, is ideal (page 43). Everyone gets to eat from the same plate at the same time, enjoying surprising pairings, discussing favorites, and rubbing elbows. The shared cheese plate is social in addition to being delicious and nutritious.

For larger parties, the shared plate may be unruly, and serving individual plates for too many people can be logistically challenging. Instead, go for a large platter during cocktail hour, before the meal. Large-format cheeses can be cut into bite-size pieces, and smaller wheels can be presented with a knife—or spoons, if that's appropriate (page 48)—so that guests can cut their own. Most likely, your guests will return to the cheese after the meal, too.

Exactly how you present your cheeses is up to you. We show many different options in this book, but only you can express your inner food stylist.

SALTED CHOCOLATE GRAHAM CRACKER

BAYLEY HAZEN BLUE, JASPER HILL FARM, VERMONT :: RAW COW'S MILK

Cheese as dessert? Yes, please! We like this pairing because it is just sweet enough to satisfy dessert lovers, but not so sweet as to turn off those who prefer to skip dessert. You can also serve it as a prelude to your dessert course. The sharp blue is mellowed by the chocolate graham cracker for an elevated dessert experience. If you like contrasts, you will love this pairing!

YIELD: 2 QUARTS

PREP TIME: 10 MINUTES

COOK TIME: 10 MINUTES PLUS 1 HOUR

12 ounces dark chocolate

2½ cups graham cracker crumbs

1½ teaspoons sea salt

Break the chocolate into small pieces, and place in the top pan of a double boiler. Fill the bottom pan of the double boiler halfway with water, and bring to a simmer. Position the top pan over the bottom pan, and stir until the chocolate is melted, about 2 to 3 minutes.

Remove the pan containing the chocolate from the heat, and add the graham cracker crumbs and salt. Mix until combined. The texture should look like wet sand.

Spread the chocolate graham on a large piece of parchment paper, at least 12 inches by 15 inches. Place another piece of parchment paper on top, and press down. Use a rolling pin to flatten the chocolate until very thin.

Place the chocolate on a baking sheet and chill for at least 1 hour or until set.

Remove the chocolate from the refrigerator. Pull off the top sheet of parchment. Flip the chocolate over and remove the second sheet of parchment. Break the chocolate up into large pieces.

Store in an airtight container in a cool place.

Chef's notes: If you are unable to find sea salt, use kosher.

Make ahead. It will keep for up to 1 month.

Other cheeses to serve with this accompaniment: Smoked ricotta, mascarpone, or a sweet blue.

Creative suggestion: Sandwich marshmallow crème between pieces of cracker for a no-heat s'more treat.

FOCUS AND BALANCE

1. Gina Marie Cream Cheese with Coconut Pineapple Cajeta (p. 166)
2. Wabash Cannonball with Fava Bean Pesto (p. 160)
3. Herdsman with Spicy Curry Cashew Brittle (p. 162)
4. Époisses with Shiitake Salad (p. 165)
5. Gorgonzola Dolce with Sweet Balsamic Pickled Figs (p. 167)

If you've been reading this book in order, you've learned a lot so far. If you haven't read it in order, which is fine, maybe you already knew a lot about cheese. Either way, you are familiar with the different styles of cheeses and the various milks from which they are made. You have considered the season, the region of the cheeses and accompaniments, who your guests are, and what your occasion is. Now it's time to start putting it all together on a plate.

When building a cheese plate there are two related objectives to consider: focus and balance.

Focus refers to the theme of the plate. Yours could be something like all Vermont cheeses (page 126), all goat's-milk cheeses (page 116–117), or all rhubarb pairings (page 108). More often, though, your focus will be *balance*, meaning that your plate will include a broad range of milks, styles, regions, and accompaniments.

Even when your focus is more specific, there is still a need for balance. For instance, if you have three rhubarb accompaniments, you will want three different rhubarb accompaniments, along with a balanced selection of cheeses. If you have five goat's-milk cheeses, you will want them to be of different styles and with a broad variety of accompaniments.

Balance should be reflected in all aspects of your cheese plate or platter. Unless your focus calls for something else, it's nice to select cheeses made from different milks, from different regions, and of different styles. It's ideal to choose accompaniments that encompass multiple ingredients, types, and flavors. For instance, unless you are focusing on nuts, it probably doesn't make sense to have two out of five pairings on a plate be cashew brittle and rosemary pine nuts.

The cheese plate we make most often at Casellula is "Five cheeses, anything goes." When the fromager gets this order, she will most likely select one cheese from each category of style (fresh, bloomy, cooked and pressed, washed, and blue) while ensuring that she ends up with the best balance of milks possible. Ideally, this will mean one each of cow, sheep, goat, and buffalo, with a mixed-milk cheese filling that fifth slot. In the United States, buffalo's-milk cheeses are hard to come by, so it is likely that one of the milks represented on the plate will appear twice.

That's enough to think about, but then she aims to balance the regions. There's no requirement, but, ideally, avoiding overlap is a goal. She will select cheeses from a few different countries in Europe, along with two cheeses from different regions of the United States. That said, it's perfectly OK to include a soft goat's-milk cheese from the Loire and an aged sheep's-milk cheese from the Jura Mountains. Sure, they're both French, but national borders are just a cultural construct, so don't worry about it.

You can see examples of plates that fulfill all or most of these ideals on pages 20–21, 44–45, and 66–67. Still, it's important for us to emphasize that finding perfect balance on the cheese plate, as in life, is an ideal to which we aspire, not a noose with which we hang ourselves. Some of our plates are a little heavy on one kind of milk (page 126) or one region (page 138–139). Sometimes the right plate doesn't hit all the category notes. That's OK. Your goal should be to make the tastiest plate possible, not to pedantically stick to the rules we've laid out in this book (see page 19). In the process, work to achieve as much balance as possible, but only insomuch as it serves the plate.

Along with balancing the cheeses, of course, we need to balance the pairings. We offer more than five categories of accompaniments, so we don't try to include them all. We aim to avoid overlapping or repeating. There's no need for two fudges, two brittles, two chutneys, or two mustards on a single plate (unless that's your focus).

For each cheese, then, our fromager is going to choose one of the several accompaniments that pair well with the cheese. Her goal is to end up with five pairings that encompass different styles, textures, and colors. Include something crunchy, something soft and spreadable, something fruity, and something pickled. Whole-grain mustards have their own texture, as do fruit curds and marshmallows. Mix it up.

Notice that we are not suggesting that each accompaniment appearing in this book is supposed to be paired with only one specific cheese. You are supposed to mix and match. For your convenience, we have created a cheese-pairing chart (page 204) that lists multiple accompaniment choices for many types of cheese, and a condiment-pairing chart (page 208) that lists multiple cheese options for each condiment recipe. At Casellula, our fromager always has lists like these to refer to, but she also has the freedom to make her own choices. You are free to do the same, as long as you aim for focus and balance.

FAVA BEAN PESTO

WABASH CANNONBALL, CAPRIOLE GOAT CHEESE, INDIANA
PASTEURIZED GOAT'S MILK

This pairing is not only delicious but also visually fetching. The bright green of the pesto jumps out against the pure-white interior of the Cannonball. We also love the light dusting of ash on the rind. Fresh fava bean pesto and tangy Wabash Cannonball will wake up your taste buds in the spring after a long cold winter.

YIELD: 2 CUPS
PREP TIME: 20 MINUTES
COOK TIME: 15 MINUTES

2 cups fresh, shelled fava beans or English peas (about 3 pounds unshelled; see Chef's Notes)

3 ounces pecorino

Zest from ½ medium lemon

½ cup extra-virgin olive oil

½ teaspoon salt

Fill a medium mixing bowl halfway with ice and place it in the freezer.

Fill a large saucepan ¾ full with water and bring to a boil. Gently add the fava beans to the boiling water. Cook for 2 minutes.

While the fava beans are cooking, remove the ice from the freezer and fill the bowl halfway with cold water.

After 2 minutes, remove the fava beans from the heat, drain, and immediately place them in the ice bath. Cool completely. Once the fava beans are cool, drain them again. Remove the thin outer skin by hand and discard.

Grate the pecorino.

Combine the fava beans in the food processor with the pecorino, lemon zest, olive oil, and salt. Purée for 15 to 20 seconds, until the ingredients are well combined but retain some texture.

Store in an airtight container. Keep refrigerated. Serve at room temperature.

Chef's notes: If you are able to find fresh fava beans or peas, they are worth the extra work. Simply feel for each bean in the pod, press on it with both thumbs, and pop it out. If you can't find fresh beans, look for frozen. Start the recipe at the blanching process. I do not recommend using dried beans.

Make ahead. It will keep for up to 1 week.

Other cheeses to serve with this accompaniment: Caña de cabra, mozzarella, or whole-milk ricotta.

Creative suggestion: Toss in a little more olive oil and a chopped bunch of fresh mint for a simple dressing for cold pasta salad.

SPICY CURRY CASHEW BRITTLE

HERDSMAN, PARISH HILL CREAMERY, VERMONT :: RAW COW'S MILK

We love the surprising ways in which brittles, with their sweetness, nuttiness, and spice, complement firm cheeses. Here, we have upped the spice quotient with a yellow curry. The crunch of the brittle plays well with the firm texture of the Herdsman. Talk to your monger about how different Alpine cheeses will call for different nuts in your brittle.

CAUTION: Hot, sticky caramel is not something you want to get on your skin. Trust me. If you are inexperienced with making caramel, I recommend wearing heavy-duty dish gloves and a long-sleeved shirt to help protect your hands and forearms.

YIELD: 2 QUARTS
PREP TIME: 10 MINUTES
COOK TIME: 30 MINUTES

3 cups unsalted cashew pieces

½ teaspoon salt

2 cups granulated sugar

1 cup light corn syrup

1 tablespoon plus 1 teaspoon Madras yellow curry powder

¼ teaspoon ground cayenne pepper

3 tablespoons unsalted butter, at room temperature

½ teaspoon baking soda

Preheat the oven to 300°F.

Spread the nuts on a baking sheet covered with a nonstick baking liner. Sprinkle the nuts evenly with the salt. Set aside.

Combine the sugar, 1 cup of water, and the corn syrup in a medium saucepan. Bring the mixture to a boil over medium heat. Continue cooking the sugar. It will thicken and change color as it cooks.

While the sugar is boiling, place the nuts in the oven to warm up, which will make it easier to spread the brittle.

Once the sugar mixture begins to change color and caramelize, reduce the heat to medium low. When the color reaches medium amber, turn off the heat.

With a heat-resistant spatula, gently stir in the curry powder, cayenne, butter, and baking soda. Mix well.

Remove the nuts from the oven and add to the caramel. Mix well.

Spread the brittle on the warm baking sheet, smoothing it out with the spatula. If the brittle seems too thick to spread, it has cooled down too much. Place the brittle in the oven for 2 minutes, remove, and try to spread again.

Let the brittle cool to room temperature in a dry place. Humidity is sugar's enemy. Once it gets in, you can't get it out.

When the brittle is cool, break it into pieces of desired size and store in an airtight container.

Chef's notes: Work quickly but carefully. The longer you stir the caramel, the cooler it will get and the harder it will be to work with.

Make ahead. It will keep for up to 1 month with no humidity.

Other cheeses to serve with this accompaniment: Gouda, dry Jack, or another firm cheese.

Creative suggestion: Chop the brittle into small pieces and bake into cookies or mix into ice cream for a great added crunch.

SHIITAKE SALAD

ÉPOISSES, FRANCE :: PASTEURIZED COW'S MILK

Époisses is a widely available stinky cheese from Burgundy. When it's young, the texture is pliant and slightly firm, but as it ages it gets funkier and more runny, even soupy. That's when you want to dive in and eat it with a spoon. This little salad is stunning to look at, and tasty, too. The mushrooms draw out the earthy notes in the cheese while the acetous vinegar and scallions balance the pungency.

YIELD: 1½ CUPS
PREP TIME: 15 MINUTES
COOK TIME: 20 MINUTES

1 pound shiitake mushrooms

4 tablespoons extra-virgin olive oil, divided

1 teaspoon salt

¼ red bell pepper

2 scallions

3 tablespoons red wine vinegar

Preheat the oven to 375°F.

Line a baking sheet with parchment paper. Set aside.

Remove the stems from the shiitakes. Discard. Slice the caps into ⅛-inch strips and place in a medium mixing bowl.

Toss the sliced mushrooms with 3 tablespoons of olive oil and salt until coated.

Spread the mushrooms evenly on the parchment-lined baking sheet. Bake until most of the mushrooms are slightly crispy and brown, about 15 to 20 minutes. Turn the baking sheet at least one time during cooking. Once they're crispy, remove from the oven and let cool to room temperature.

Finely dice the red pepper.

Slice the green tops of the scallions into very thin rounds, discarding the white bottoms.

Place the mushrooms back in the mixing bowl with the red pepper, scallions, vinegar, and the remaining 1 tablespoon of olive oil. Toss to coat the mushrooms evenly.

Store the mushrooms in an airtight container and keep refrigerated. Serve at room temperature.

Chef's note: Make ahead. It will keep for up to 3 days.

Other cheeses to serve with this accompaniment: Halloumi, Jasper Hill Willoughby, or Chiriboga Blue.

Creative suggestions: Try this salad with a cheese omelet for breakfast, or use it as a different kind of taco topping.

Focus and Balance

COCONUT PINEAPPLE CAJETA

GINA MARIE CREAM CHEESE, SIERRA NEVADA CHEESE CO., CALIFORNIA
PASTEURIZED COW'S MILK

The simple combination of lush cultured cream cheese with a kiss of tropical sauce instantly whisks away your taste buds on a first-class flight to the Caribbean islands. If only your body were invited.

YIELD: 1½ CUPS
PREP TIME: 5 MINUTES
COOK TIME: 1 HOUR

1 vanilla bean

2 cans unsweetened coconut milk

1 cup pineapple juice

1 cup granulated sugar

½ teaspoon baking soda

Cut the vanilla bean in half lengthwise with the tip of a paring knife. Reserve half the bean for another use. Scrape out the seeds using the tip of the knife, dragging from one end of the bean to the other.

In a large pot, bring the coconut milk, pineapple juice, sugar, and vanilla to a boil. Once at a boil, turn off the heat.

Dilute the baking soda in 1 tablespoon of warm water, and then stir it into the coconut milk mixture. The mixture will instantly rise. Turn the heat to low and cook, stirring, until it no longer rises.

Increase the heat to medium and continue to cook, stirring occasionally, until thick, about 1 hour. Remove from the heat and let cool.

Store in an airtight container, refrigerated. Serve at room temperature.

Chef's note: Make ahead. It will keep for up to 2 weeks.

Other cheeses to serve with this accompaniment: A young, sweet, creamy cheese like ricotta, quark, or mascarpone.

Creative suggestion: Mix a bit of this cajeta into your cream cheese frosting for a tropical twist.

SWEET BALSAMIC PICKLED FIGS

GORGONZOLA DOLCE, ITALY :: PASTEURIZED COW'S MILK

Gorgonzola dolce (also called Gorgonzola cremificato) is a sweeter, creamier version of Gorgonzola piccante. This is a great cheese for people who think they don't like blues. When paired with the dark, aromatic, sweet pickled figs, it has a dessert-like quality. Consider serving this combination at the end of your meal.

YIELD: 3 CUPS

PREP TIME: 20 MINUTES

COOK TIME: 35 MINUTES

TOTAL TIME: 2 DAYS

8 ounces dried figs (preferably Black Mission)

1 medium orange

1 stick cinnamon

2 whole cloves

1 teaspoon black pepper

½ cup balsamic vinegar

8 ounces granulated sugar

Chef's note: Make ahead. They will keep for up to 2 weeks.

Other cheeses to serve with this accompaniment: Pecorino ginepro, Stilton, or Parish Hill West West Blue.

Creative suggestions: These are great served with vanilla ice cream or on top of a prosciutto, ricotta, and arugula sandwich.

Cut the tips of the stems off the figs and discard. Place the figs in a heat-proof bowl.

Bring 2 cups water to a boil. Pour the water over the figs and let cool to room temperature.

Drain the figs and discard the liquid. Cut the figs in half lengthwise. Set aside.

Using a vegetable peeler, remove the zest from half the orange, creating long strips. Reserve the orange for another use.

Place the orange zest, cinnamon stick, cloves, and black pepper in a 6 x 6-inch piece of cheesecloth. Gather the corners and tie closed with cooking twine. This is called a sachet.

In a medium saucepan, bring the balsamic vinegar, sugar, ½ cup water, and the sachet to a boil. Cook, stirring constantly, until all the sugar is dissolved, about 10 minutes.

Add the figs and boil on low heat for 5 minutes, stirring occasionally.

Pour the figs and liquid into a pickling jar and refrigerate for at least 12 hours or overnight.

The next day, strain the liquid into a small saucepan. Reserve the figs. Bring the liquid to a boil over medium heat. Add the figs and cook on low for 5 minutes.

Return the figs and liquid to the jar and refrigerate for at least 12 hours or overnight.

Keep refrigerated until ready to serve. Serve at room temperature.

1. Green Dirt Farm's Fresh Spreadable Sheep's Milk Cheese with Kale Pesto (p. 175)
2. Gruyère with Castelvetrano Olive Lemon Tapenade (p. 173)
3. Frère Fumant with Sweet and Sour Pineapple (p. 176)
4. Dancing Fern with Golden Cauliflower Purée (p. 178)
5. Grevenbroeker with Green Tea White Chocolate Fudge (p. 179)

You've thought about what you want on your plate, so now it's time to consider how you are going to present your cheeses and accompaniments. You can keep it simple and use a plate or platter you already own, or you can go searching for exactly the right piece for your concept.

At Casellula, we serve our cheeses on rectangular white plates. The rim helps to hold some of our looser condiments in place, and the colors of the condiments pop against the white. We present the cheeses and accompaniments from left to right, mildest to strongest. The reasoning for this is simple. If you put a strong blue or a stinky washed rind on your tongue first, you are not going to be able to taste the light, fresh goat's-milk cheese that you try after it.

For the last several years, serving cheese on slate has become common. Slate offers the fun advantage of your being able to write the names of the cheeses on it with chalk, and the dark slate provides a nice contrast for the white and yellow of the cheeses. On the other hand, everyone is doing it. Only you know if that makes it right for you, or so very wrong.

To a certain extent, the size and shape of your plate, platter, or board will dictate how the cheese is presented. Cheeses have been served in a circle for years, starting at twelve o'clock and going clockwise around the plate, mildest to strongest, probably because plates are traditionally round. Americans typically have included only one accompaniment on a plate of various cheeses, probably because that's all that would fit in the middle of the round plate filled with cheeses. You can do better than that.

Don't limit yourself to what we do (white rectangles) or to what so many others do (slate). Instead, be creative and find other surfaces. Woods and bamboos, which you can find in the form of good-quality cutting boards, work beautifully for larger cheese platters or small individual servings. Antique cutting boards, plates, serving platters, pieces of marble, granite, or simple planks of wood can be beautiful.

There is a lot of fun to be had with presenting the condiments, too. Many can be simply placed on the plate. Some can be shaped into quenelles (page 138 and page 156) or just spooned (page 96). Others require a vessel of some kind. Be creative. You can use simple round ramekins to hold liquids (page 20–21), as well as small pitchers, cups, or anything else you can imagine.

Choosing the order for the cheeses is not so simple. There can be disagreement, even among professionals, as to the order in which the cheeses should be placed. They should go from mildest to strongest, but most cheeses are neither extremely mild nor extremely strong but are somewhere in the middle. Should the fresh crottin come before the stinky chällerhocker? Absolutely. But should the Emmentaler come before or after the Vermont Shepherd? That's anybody's call. In some cases, as with very pungent washed-rind cheeses, a blue may not be the last on the plate.

The order on the plate is further complicated by the condiments. Generally, one doesn't want to coat one's palate with sugar before tasting savory flavors. (That is why drinking soda with a good meal is a travesty.) Sometimes, however, we pair fudge or some other slightly sweet condiment with a mild cheese. It's a conundrum—you shouldn't eat the candy before the pesto, but you shouldn't have the Époisses before the Chabichou.

So what do we do? We say don't worry about it. You should present the cheeses in an order that makes sense and can be explained, but don't split hairs. All those cheeses of moderate strength in the middle of the plate can go in whatever order you are comfortable with. If you need to, you can use the condiment as a tiebreaker.

You may also, especially with large platters, disregard the order. You can put the cheeses and accompaniments in an attractive layout on a platter that is neither a line nor a circle (page 66–67). You are creative that way. You can split up a large platter on multiple, smaller surfaces, as we've done on page 44–45. You can even spread them out around the house so that one plate is in the living room and another in the kitchen, encouraging your guests to move around the party.

In practice, almost no one eats each cheese with its condiment in its entirety before moving on to the next. Most people will try each cheese, decide what

Presentation

their favorites are, and then bounce around from cheese to cheese. It's all right with us.

What about the cheese itself? Cheeses can be presented in so many different ways. Hard cheeses can be cut into cubes, matchsticks, or pie shapes. Soft cheeses can be spooned out or spread on bread. Others may be cut into wedges or crumbled into chunks.

You have probably noticed from the photos in this book that we love a pie-shaped wedge. You can see how we do that in the cutting guide (page 202). This is not just for aesthetics. Cheeses age differently on the outside than they do on the inside, so the flavor of any given cheese is different close to the center than it is near the rind. The pie-shaped portion includes paste from the center, the rind, and everything in between. The fact that it looks cute on the plate is just lucky.

With very large wheels of cheese it is a little unwieldy to get center and rind in one reasonably sized portion. A wheel of Comté, for instance, is upwards of eighty pounds and about two feet in diameter. Some cheeses are even bigger. In those cases, you are going to buy a wedge that represents only a small section of the whole wheel. Cut the cheese into half-ounce to one-ounce portions in whatever way suits your presentation. We like matchsticks (page 85), which are symmetrical and stackable (and actually larger than real matchsticks), but we are also happy to crumble up a hard cheese so the portions are randomly sized and shaped (page 84). Cubes just remind us of bad cheese boards filled with grocery store Cheddar that our parents put out at parties in the '70s and '80s, so we don't go there. But there are no rules, so we can't stop you from doing whatever suits you.

Your cheese presentation should be beautiful to look at and fun to eat. You want to aim for variety in how your cheeses are cut and how the accompaniments are presented. Various colors and textures are also nice. Although it is good to balance the flavors and styles and present them in a logical order (mildest to strongest, more or less), the most important thing about the presentation is that it is yours!

CASTELVETRANO OLIVE LEMON TAPENADE

GRUYÈRE EIGHTEEN MONTH, GOURMINO, SWITZERLAND
RAW COW'S MILK

Gruyère is one of the oldest cheeses on the block, and it deserves to be paired with one of the oldest fruits known to man—the olive! Meaty, big Castelvetrano olives pair well with the nutty, salty Gruyère because of their naturally crisp, fresh, bright flesh.

YIELD: 2 CUPS
PREP TIME: 10 MINUTES

Grated zest from 1 lemon

3 cups pitted Castelvetrano olives

½ cup extra-virgin olive oil

½ teaspoon black pepper

Place the lemon zest, olives, oil, and black pepper in a food processor. Purée until smooth and blended, about 2 minutes. Scrape down the sides once while processing.

Store the tapenade in an airtight container. Keep refrigerated. Serve at room temperature.

Chef's note: Make ahead. It will keep for up to 2 weeks.

Other cheeses to serve with this accompaniment: Comté, Jarlsberg, or a savory blue.

Creative suggestion: Stuff the tapenade inside a chicken breast for a flavorful, moist roast.

KALE PESTO

Green Dirt Farm's Fresh Spreadable Sheep's Milk Cheese is as clean and tasty as any fresh sheep's-milk cheese you will find. Spread it on bread or bagels, or eat it with fresh fruit. Here, we've made a little crostini topped with Fresh and kale pesto. You can use any good fresh cheese if you don't have access to the Fresh from Green Dirt Farm—ricotta or chèvre will do the trick.

YIELD: 2 CUPS
PREP TIME: 10 MINUTES
COOK TIME: 20 MINUTES

1 bunch curly kale

4 ounces pecorino

1 garlic clove

1 cup extra-virgin olive oil

1 teaspoon salt

Chef's note: Make ahead. It will keep for up to 1 week.

Other cheeses to serve with this accompaniment: San Andreas, pecorino, or provolone.

Creative suggestion: Mix this pesto into hummus for an even healthier snack.

Fill a medium mixing bowl halfway with ice and place in the freezer.

Fill a large saucepan ¾ full with water and bring to a boil.

Remove the stems from the kale and discard. Tear the leaves into medium pieces. They need not be perfectly uniform, but tearing them makes them easier to purée later.

Remove the ice from the freezer and fill the bowl halfway with cold water.

Gently lower the kale into the boiling water and cook for 1½ minutes. Drain the kale and immediately place it in the ice bath. Cool completely.

Once the kale is cool, drain it again, pressing out as much liquid as possible. Wrap the kale in a cloth towel (it should be a towel you don't mind staining) and squeeze out as much water as possible.

Grate the pecorino on the largest hole on a box grater.

Place the kale in a food processor with the pecorino, garlic, olive oil, and salt. Purée for 15 to 30 seconds, or until all is combined and smooth.

Store in an airtight container. Keep refrigerated. Serve at room temperature.

SWEET AND SOUR PINEAPPLE

FRÈRE FUMANT, 3-CORNER FIELD FARM, NEW YORK :: RAW SHEEP'S MILK

This sweet, sour, savory, and salty pineapple is reminiscent of a zesty BBQ sauce and cries out for something smoked. Frère fumant, a sheep's-milk cheese from upstate New York, answers its call. It's made in the style of Idiazabal, from the Basque region of Spain, and is cold-smoked at a local monastery. The name means "smoking brother." Get it?

YIELD: 2 CUPS
PREP TIME: 20 MINUTES
COOK TIME: 40 MINUTES

1 cup pineapple juice

2 garlic cloves

¼ teaspoon red chili flakes

1½ teaspoons cornstarch

½ cup ketchup

½ cup light brown sugar

1 tablespoon Sriracha

⅓ cup white vinegar

2 tablespoons soy sauce

2 tablespoons sesame oil

1 ripe pineapple

In a blender, purée the pineapple juice, garlic, chili flakes, and cornstarch on high speed until smooth, about 1 minute.

Combine the purée in a medium saucepan with the ketchup, brown sugar, Sriracha, vinegar, soy sauce, and sesame oil. Cook over medium heat, constantly stirring, until the sauce boils. Boil for 1 minute.

Remove the sauce from the heat and let cool. Set aside.

Preheat the oven to 375°F.

Line a baking sheet with a nonstick baking liner.

Trim the top and outer layer from the pineapple. Cut off the four sides lengthwise from around the core. Discard the core. Slice the flesh into ¼-inch pieces and arrange them on the baking sheet.

Using a pastry brush, brush the tops of the pineapple slices with the sweet and sour sauce.

Bake the pineapple for 10 minutes. Remove from the oven and turn over each piece. Brush with the sweet and sour sauce. Bake for another 10 minutes. Repeat the turning and basting process. Continue baking, turning and basting every 10 minutes, for a total baking time of 40 minutes, or until the pineapple slices have nicely toasted, sticky edges.

Remove from the oven and let cool. Store in an airtight container. Keep refrigerated. Serve at room temperature or warm.

Chef's note: Make ahead. They will keep for up to 5 days.

Other cheeses to serve with this accompaniment: Ibores, Idiazabal, or Grafton Maple Smoked Cheddar.

Creative suggestion: Take your Hawaiian pizza to the next level by adding this in place of plain pineapple.

Presentation

GOLDEN CAULIFLOWER PURÉE

DANCING FERN, SEQUATCHIE COVE CREAMERY, TENNESSEE
RAW COW'S MILK

Turmeric is a spice that is gaining popularity as a healthy addition to foods. You can take advantage of its health benefits and create a warm visual while using up that jar that has been sitting in your pantry. In the last few years, Sequatchie Cove has emerged as one of the premier artisan cheese makers in the country. Based on a French Reblochon, Dancing Fern can be like smooth, thick pudding or downright runny.

YIELD: 2 CUPS
PREP TIME: 5 MINUTES
COOK TIME: 20 MINUTES

1 head cauliflower

3 tablespoons unsalted butter

1 tablespoon extra-virgin olive oil

2 teaspoons turmeric

2 teaspoons salt

Trim the cauliflower to remove the green leaves and stem. Discard the trimmings. Chop the cauliflower into small florets, about 1 inch each.

Place the butter, olive oil, ½ cup of water, and cauliflower in a medium saucepan. Cover with a lid or aluminum foil. Cook over medium heat for about 15 minutes, or until the cauliflower is soft.

Remove the cauliflower from the heat and place it in a blender. Add the turmeric, salt, and ¼ cup water. Purée on high speed for 2 minutes, or until smooth. Make sure to scrape down the sides.

Store in an airtight container. Keep refrigerated. Serve at room temperature.

Chef's notes: If you do not have turmeric, you can omit it.

Make ahead. It will keep for up to 1 week.

Other cheeses that go well with this accompaniment: Vulto Ouleout, Taleggio, or a savory, soft cow's-milk cheese.

Creative suggestion: Scrape the purée into an ovenproof dish, top with seasoned bread crumbs, and pop it in the oven for 20 to 30 minutes for an easy baked side dish.

GREEN TEA WHITE CHOCOLATE FUDGE

GREVENBROEKER, BELGIUM :: PASTEURIZED COW'S MILK

The bright green color of this fudge jumps off the plate. Grevenbroeker is layered by hand, with the mold sprinkled between the large curds so that it grows along the borders, giving the cheese the look of marble. This is one of our favorite pairings both to taste and to look at.

YIELD: ABOUT 1 POUND
PREP TIME: 10 MINUTES
COOK TIME: 15 MINUTES PLUS 4 HOURS

12 ounces white chocolate

8 ounces cream cheese, at room temperature

2 tablespoons unsalted butter, at room temperature

3 cups confectioners' sugar

1 tablespoon green tea matcha powder

1 teaspoon vanilla extract

Pinch of salt

Break the chocolate into small pieces and place in a small mixing bowl or the top pan of a double boiler. Fill the bottom of the double boiler with water and bring to a simmer. Set the pan or bowl containing the chocolate over the top of the double boiler. Cook, stirring, until melted, about 2 to 3 minutes. Remove the chocolate from the heat and set aside.

In a medium mixing bowl stir together the cream cheese, butter, sugar, green tea, vanilla, and salt until smooth. Add the melted white chocolate and mix until combined.

Pour the fudge into a 6 x 6-inch baking pan lined with plastic wrap or a flexible mold of your choice. Chill for at least 4 hours or until set.

Remove the fudge from the pan by lifting up the edges of the plastic wrap. Remove the plastic and cut the fudge into the desired size.

Keep refrigerated in an airtight container. Serve chilled or at room temperature.

Chef's notes: You may substitute the white chocolate with milk chocolate or dark chocolate.

Make ahead. It will keep for up to 2 weeks.

Other cheeses to serve with this accompaniment: La Tur, BoxCarr Farm Rosie's Robiola and mild, sweet blues.

Creative suggestions: Play around with the flavors for the fudge. Add 2 tablespoons lemon zest and 2 teaspoons of poppy seeds for another visually appealing and tasty creation.

Presentation

HOW TO WRAP AND STORE CHEESE

1. Mozzarella with Tomato Confit (p. 184)
2. Green Hill with Creamed Corn (p. 190)
3. Quicke's Vintage Cheddar with Bacon Love (p. 186)
4. Marieke Premium Gouda with Orange Confit (p. 189)
5. Dunbarton Blue with Sweet and Spicy Apple Chutney (p. 191)

In your effort to keep your cheeses at their best for the longest period of time, there are a few concerns to keep in mind.

Cheese is a sponge. It will absorb the flavors and smells of whatever is around it, so one of your main goals is to protect it from other things. Cheese left unwrapped in a refrigerator will start to smell like refrigerator.

Cheese gets dry over time. You can control this loss of moisture expensively, by installing a humidity control system in your home, or simply, by wrapping the cheese and storing it near a damp towel or humidor stone.

Some cheeses, like many other foods, can harbor contaminants that will grow at room temperature, so they should be refrigerated to prevent that.

The solutions to all these problems are the same: wrapping and refrigerating. Each wrap has its advantages and disadvantages.

Plastic wrap is the most convenient (and therefore the most common) way to store cheese, but most cheeses will, over time, absorb a little cling-wrap flavor from the direct contact. Plus, cheese can't breathe through plastic, so it will suffocate. If you are storing a cheese for more than twenty-four hours, we advise against plastic wrap. Notice, however, that most cheese shops store their cheese by wrapping it in plastic, even in France. This should give you an idea of how (not) big a deal it is for the short term. Alternatively, you can wrap your blues in aluminum foil and your hard cheeses in waxed paper.

Specially designed cheese paper, available online or at most good cheese shops, is better. It protects the cheese, and it has microperforations that allow the cheese to breathe, albeit slightly. On the downside, it is not airtight, so the onion in the crisper may affect the cheese. You can control this by first wrapping the cheese in cheese paper then placing it in an airtight container. A fancy package of cheese paper makes a great gift.

The best way to store cheese, in our experience, is by creating microclimates for each cheese. Professionals do this by having multiple "caves" (otherwise known as walk-in refrigerators), each with a set temperature and humidity level, each type of cheese segregated from the others. This way, blues get the high humidity they need without getting blue mold all up in the rinds of other cheeses, older cheeses get a lower humidity, and so on.

You can do something similar in your home refrigerator by using sealable plastic or glass storage containers. You can also recycle plastic takeout boxes from restaurants, but make sure they are clean and free of remnant odors. These sealed containers protect the cheese completely from other smells and flavors while providing little direct contact with the cheese, so the protection itself doesn't affect the flavor. They offer room for a little air to move around the cheese, so the cheese can breathe. Ideally, the container should be just big enough to fit the cheese. If you put a damp paper towel, rolled up or folded, in the container with the cheese you can increase the humidity, which is a great way to prevent soft cheeses from drying out. You could even go the extra step and use a humidor brick or stone instead of a wet paper towel.

Cheese should be served at room temperature, so when you take a cheese out of the refrigerator, let it temper for at least an hour before serving. If the outside edges look a little dry, or have plastic wrap patterns, you can "face" the cheese by scraping or cutting off a thin layer.

As for temperature, you are not aging the cheese, you are storing it, so it should be kept in a refrigerator set below 42°F (but above freezing). This is true for every cheese that requires refrigeration and is acceptable even for those that don't. Just be sure to take your cheese out of the fridge and let it set to room temperature before you eat it!

TOMATO CONFIT

FRESH MOZZARELLA, MOZZARELLA COMPANY, TEXAS
PASTEURIZED COW'S MILK

Paula Lambert, of Mozzarella Company in Dallas, Texas, has been making these beauties since 1982. Mozzarella is intended to be eaten immediately after being made, so you should find the best mozzarella available in your area. It may be locally produced so that you can purchase and eat it the day it was made, or it may be flown in from Italy. Playing on the classic Italian caprese salad, we have paired the mozzarella with tomato confit. You may want to one-up us and add some fresh basil leaves to your plate.

YIELD: 1 CUP
PREP TIME: 1 HOUR
COOK TIME: 1 HOUR PLUS 20 MINUTES

6 ripe plum tomatoes

2 teaspoons extra-virgin olive oil

2 sprigs fresh thyme, leaves removed from stems and stems discarded

½ sprig fresh rosemary, leaves removed from stem and stem discarded

1 teaspoon salt

¼ teaspoon ground black pepper

Preheat the oven to 300°F.

Fill a medium mixing bowl halfway with ice and place in the freezer.

Fill a large saucepan ¾ full with water and bring to a boil.

Using the tip of a paring knife, cut about an inch into the stem end of each tomato, angling inward. Circle the stem with your knife, and remove and discard the core. Cut a small X on the other end of each tomato, about ½ inch by ½ inch.

Remove the ice from the freezer and fill the bowl halfway with cold water.

Gently lower the tomatoes into the boiling water. Boil the tomatoes for 2 minutes. You will start to see the skin peeling away where you cut the X's.

Remove the tomatoes from the boiling water and immediately place them in the ice bath. Cool completely. Once cool, remove them from the ice bath.

Peel the tomatoes using a paring knife. Discard the skin. On a cutting board, cut the tomatoes lengthwise into quarters. Remove and discard the seeds. If the seeds are not easily removed by hand, you can cut them out with your paring knife.

Combine the tomatoes in a medium mixing bowl with the remaining ingredients. Toss to coat the tomatoes.

Arrange the tomatoes evenly on a baking sheet lined with parchment paper. Bake for 45 minutes to 1 hour, rotating the baking sheet halfway through. The juices from the tomatoes will be browned on the parchment, but the tomatoes should still be moist and red.

Remove from the oven and let cool to room temperature.

Place the tomatoes in an airtight container and drizzle 2 teaspoons olive oil over the top. Cover. Keep refrigerated. Serve at room temperature or warm.

Chef's note: Make ahead. They will keep for up to 1 week.

Other cheeses to serve with this accompaniment: Parmigiano-Reggiano, Manchego, or another firm, aged cheese.

Creative suggestions: Tomato confit is a versatile ingredient and a great addition to any sandwich, salad, or burger.

BACON LOVE

VINTAGE CHEDDAR, QUICKE'S, UNITED KINGDOM
PASTEURIZED COW'S MILK

Most people have a big love affair with bacon, and most cheese lovers have a big love for Cheddar, which makes this one of the best crowd-pleasing pairings in the book. It is sure to please just about anyone! Quicke's Vintage Cheddar is clothbound and aged for two years. The pleasant horseradish tang of the cheese helps cut through the delicious fat in the pairing.

YIELD: 1 CUP
PREP TIME: 5 MINUTES
COOK TIME: 20 MINUTES

9 ounces sliced smoked bacon

¼ cup plus 2 tablespoons molasses

¼ cup light brown sugar

1 teaspoon onion powder

¼ teaspoon cayenne pepper

Pinch of salt

Cut the bacon into ¼-inch pieces. In a medium saucepan, cook the bacon over medium heat, stirring occasionally, until crispy, about 15 minutes.

Turn the heat to low and add the molasses, brown sugar, onion powder, cayenne, and salt. Cook, stirring, until all the fat is emulsified, about 1 minute. This will happen as the liquid returns to a boil.

Turn off the heat and stir in ¼ cup water until combined.

Let cool until warm before transferring to an airtight container. Keep refrigerated. Serve at room temperature.

Chef's note: Make ahead. It will keep for up to 1 week.

Other cheeses to serve with this accompaniment: Clothbound Cheddars aged a minimum of 18 months, soft washed-rinds, or a strong blue.

Creative suggestions: Spread on toast for breakfast, use as a decadent topping on a burger, or sandwich between peanut butter cookies for a sinful sweet treat.

ORANGE CONFIT

PREMIUM GOUDA 18 MONTH, MARIEKE GOUDA, WISCONSIN
RAW COW'S MILK

Attention sweet-tooths! Orange confit with aged Marieke Gouda may make you feel like a kid in a candy shop. The Gouda is fudgy, sweet, and salty, and it pairs beautifully with the orange confit, which rounds things out with its bright, citrusy flavor.

YIELD: 2 CUPS

PREP TIME: 15 MINUTES

COOK TIME: 1½ HOURS

4 medium navel oranges

3 cups granulated sugar

Pinch of salt

Cut the oranges in half parallel to the ends. Squeeze as much juice out as possible. Reserve the juice.

Using a spoon, scoop out the flesh of each orange to remove it from the rind. Discard. Cut the rind in half, and slice into ¼-inch-thick strips.

Fill a medium saucepan with water and bring to a boil. Place the orange-rind strips in the water and blanch for 3 minutes. Strain the rinds, discarding the water. Repeat the blanching process two more times.

After the third blanching, combine the orange rinds, juice, sugar, salt, and 2 cups of water in the pot. Boil over medium heat until the liquid becomes syrupy and thick, about 30 to 45 minutes, or until it reaches 238°F on a thermometer. Remove from the heat and let cool for 20 minutes.

Store in an airtight container. Keep refrigerated. Serve cold or at room temperature.

Chef's note: Make ahead. It will keep for up to 1 month.

Other cheeses to serve with this accompaniment: Red Hawk, ricotta, or a washed sheep's-milk cheese.

Creative suggestion: Add a spoonful to your bagel with cream cheese for a bright morning.

How to Wrap and Store Cheese

CREAMED CORN

GREEN HILL, SWEET GRASS DAIRY, GEORGIA :: PASTEURIZED COW'S MILK

Green Hill tastes like buttery, creamy summer-corn pudding! We decided to double down by pairing it with exactly those flavors. This creamed corn includes just a few simple ingredients, so what you taste will be the good-quality butter and the ripe sweet corn.

YIELD: 2 CUPS
PREP TIME: 10 MINUTES
COOK TIME: 10 MINUTES

3 ears fresh sweet corn

4 ounces unsalted butter

1 teaspoon salt

½ teaspoon black pepper

2 tablespoons heavy cream

2 tablespoons finely chopped fresh chives

Remove the husks from the cob and discard.

Lay a corn cob on the cutting board, and trim off the butt end to create a flat bottom. Repeat with each cob. Now stand the cob upright on its end and carefully cut the corn off. Once nearly all the corn is removed, use the spine of the knife blade to scrape the few remaining kernels off the cob. Repeat with each cob.

In a medium saucepan, combine the butter and corn. Cook over medium heat until the corn is soft and plump, stirring occasionally, about 5 to 6 minutes. Season with the salt and pepper. Remove from the heat.

Place the cream and about a third of the corn in a blender, and purée on high until smooth, adding a bit more cream if necessary. Transfer the puréed corn back to the saucepan and stir together with the remaining corn.

Fold the chives into the corn.

Transfer to an airtight container and cool. Keep refrigerated. Let it come to room temperature and stir before serving.

Chef's notes: If you are unable to use fresh corn, substitute frozen.

Make ahead. It will keep for up to 5 days.

Other cheeses to serve with this accompaniment: Brillat-Savarin, Brie, or a bloomy-rind cheese.

Creative suggestion: This creamed corn would be a delicious addition to a savory waffle. Grate some Cheddar on top!

SWEET AND SPICY APPLE CHUTNEY

DUNBARTON BLUE, ROELLI CHEESE HAUS, WISCONSIN

PASTEURIZED COW'S MILK

Dunbarton Blue is one of our favorite American cheeses to emerge in the last few years, in part because it is a great entry-level blue. It is pierced to allow oxygen in so the blue mold will grow, and then it is pressed, limiting the oxygen and therefore the amount of blue. The end result (see page 181) is a cheese that has flavor notes of Cheddar, with a taste of blue that is not too aggressive. The apple chutney balances that sharp kiss of blue with a sweet and spicy hug.

YIELD: 3 CUPS
PREP TIME: 20 MINUTES
COOK TIME: 45 MINUTES

- 2 cups cider vinegar
- 2 cups light brown sugar
- 5 garlic cloves
- 2 ounces fresh ginger, peeled and sliced or coarsely chopped
- 1½ teaspoons salt
- 1 teaspoon red chili flakes
- 2 pounds Granny Smith apples
- 1½ cups golden raisins
- 2 sticks cinnamon
- 2 tablespoons yellow mustard seeds

Place the vinegar, brown sugar, garlic, ginger, salt, and red chili flakes in the blender. Purée on medium-high until smooth, about 1 minute.

Peel the apples with a vegetable peeler and cut out the core. Discard the core. Dice the apples into ¼-inch-thick cubes. They need not be perfectly uniform.

Place the apples, raisins, cinnamon, and mustard seeds in a large saucepan. Pour the vinegar blend over the apples. Simmer, stirring occasionally, over medium heat until almost all the liquid has reduced, about 25 to 30 minutes.

Remove the cinnamon sticks. Turn off the heat and let cool.

Store in an airtight container. Keep refrigerated. Serve cold, warm, or at room temperature.

Chef's note: Make ahead. It will keep for up to 2 weeks.

Other cheeses to serve with this accompaniment: Parish Hill Herdsman, San Joaquin Gold, or a fruity washed rind.

Creative suggestions: Serve this chutney with grilled pork chops or a roast ham. You may play around with the spices depending on the season. Try adding some ground clove, nutmeg, or allspice during the holidays.

LET'S EAT!

1. **Georgic with Brandy Poached Pears (p. 196)**
2. **Anton's Ziege Rot with Lush Leeks (p. 195)**
3. **San Andreas with Pineapple Mostarda (p. 198)**
4. **Taleggio with Broccoli Anchovy Purée (p. 199)**
5. **La Peral with Sweet Pickled Concord Grapes (p. 201)**

You've put a lot work into creating your beautiful cheese presentation, so now you get to enjoy it with your friends! Luckily, there is no right or wrong way to eat a cheese plate, but of course we have some simple suggestions.

Cheeses should always be served at room temperature. Take your cheeses out of the refrigerator about an hour before serving.

You should, as a general rule, plate your cheeses with the rinds included. Chances are the rinds—which, as you know by now, usually consist of mold— were intended to be eaten. They add positive elements to the experience: texture, flavor, and intensity. Rinds are often more pungent than the paste in the middle of a wheel of cheese, so some people may not like some rinds. That's OK. Let all your guests see the cheese on the plate as it was made, taste the rind, and decide for themselves whether they like it. If they don't like the rind, they don't have to eat anymore of it. But our guess is that they probably will.

You should start by tasting the mildest cheeses first. Then move on to the more intense flavors of the washed-rind and blue cheeses. In general, that means tasting in the order of the categories: fresh, soft and bloomy, cooked and pressed, washed, and blue.

Taste the cheese by itself first, then taste the cheese with its accompaniment, and see how one affects the other. Sometimes the flavors will complement and other times they will contrast. Texture adds to the experience, too. Next, take a sip of your beverage to see how it changes the experience of the cheese with the pairing and to cleanse your palate.

Move on to the next cheese. Repeat until you have tasted them all.

Now it's a free-for-all. Go back to the combinations you liked the best. Sample cheeses with different accompaniments, and think about how disparate flavors affect each other. Keep taking sips of your beverage between tastes to cleanse the palate.

Remember, cheese plates are social. Discuss the pairings with your friends. Find out what surprising combination someone else has liked, and try it yourself.

Don't be afraid to argue. If you all agree on what you like and dislike, then your cheese plate is too easy. At Casellula, we like to challenge our guests to expand their horizons. We believe that if you like every pairing on your plate, then we have failed to push you far enough. Try a stinky cheese with various pairings until you find the one that balances the stink. Try a mild blue, and work your way to stronger ones. Spread the cheese on bread or a cracker to further cut the strength.

By now you should be comfortable with everything you need to know, from how to consider the season when choosing your accompaniments, to working with your cheesemonger to find just the right cheeses, to how to present them. Now you, your friends, and your family get to enjoy the fruits (and vegetables) of your labor. Congratulations! It's time to pour yourself a drink, relax, and enjoy your cheese plate!

LUSH LEEKS

ANTON'S ZIEGE ROT, KÄSEREI ZURWIES, BAVARIA
PASTEURIZED GOAT'S MILK

Anton makes stunning Bavarian beauties with organic milk from local dairies. He is also known for his witty labels, which feature his daughters in traditional dress feeding him cheese. These lush leeks complement the complex, slightly pungent, herbaceous flavors in this rare cheese.

YIELD: 2 CUPS
PREP TIME: 10 MINUTES
COOK TIME: 15 MINUTES

3 leeks

2 ounces unsalted butter

½ cup heavy cream

1½ teaspoons salt

Trim off the dark green tops of the leeks, keeping the white and light green parts. Reserve the tops for homemade vegetable broth. Trim off and discard the roots. Slice the leeks in half lengthwise. Rinse them to remove any dirt or sand between the layers, but make sure to keep the layers together. Slice them into ¼-inch-thick half-moons.

In a medium saucepan, melt the butter over medium heat until hot; be careful not to let it brown. Add the leeks and cook until limp and slightly translucent, about 10 minutes.

Add the heavy cream and salt. Continue to cook over medium heat for another 5 minutes. The cream will reduce, creating a thick sauce. Turn off the heat and let cool.

Store in an airtight container. Keep refrigerated. Bring the leeks to room temperature before serving, or slightly warm them to create a smooth consistency.

Chef's note: Make ahead. They will keep for up to 3 days.

Other cheeses to serve with this accompaniment: Taleggio, Muenster, or Havarti.

Creative suggestion: Mix the leeks into rice as a creamy side dish for any meal.

Let's Eat!

BRANDY POACHED PEARS

GEORGIC, CALKINS CREAMERY, PENNSYLVANIA :: PASTEURIZED COW'S MILK

Georgic, from Calkins Creamery, is quark, a smooth, fresh cheese similar to fromage blanc. Brandy-poached pears are a delicious and simple pairing. Think about serving this at a fall brunch or as a simple dessert with candied nuts.

YIELD: 12 PEARS
PREP TIME: 15 MINUTES
COOK TIME: 1 HOUR

12 Seckel pears
1 medium lemon
1 vanilla bean
½ cup pear brandy (e.g., poire Williams)
1½ cups sweet white wine (e.g., riesling)
1½ cups light brown sugar
2 pods star anise

Peel the pears using a vegetable peeler, leaving the stem on. Cut the pears in half lengthwise, including the stems. Scoop out the seeds using a melon baller or small spoon. Discard the seeds.

Using the vegetable peeler, remove the zest from half the lemon, forming long strips. Reserve the lemon for another use.

Cut the vanilla bean in half lengthwise with the tip of a paring knife. Reserve half the bean for another use. Scrape out the seeds using the tip of the knife, dragging from one end to the other.

In a medium saucepan, bring the brandy, wine, brown sugar, vanilla seeds and bean, lemon peel, star anise, and 3 cups of water to a boil. Continue to boil for 5 minutes to cook off some of the alcohol.

Reduce the heat to a simmer. Gently lower the pears into the poaching liquid. Poach the pears, stirring about every 15 minutes, for 45 minutes to 1 hour. The pears should be soft but not overcooked. When you pierce a pear with a paring knife, it should come out easily.

Remove the saucepan from the heat. Gently remove the pears from the liquid using a slotted spoon, and place on a plate. Chill the pears until cool. Place the cooled pears in an airtight container and cover with the poaching liquid.

Keep refrigerated. Serve cold, warm, or at room temperature.

Chef's notes: If you are unable to find Seckel pears, you may use a firm pear such as Bosc.

Make ahead. They will keep for up to 1 week.

Other cheeses to serve with this accompaniment: Cayuga Blue, mascarpone, or Fontina.

Creative suggestions: These pears are excellent served hollowed out and filled with a mild, creamy blue cheese. Or you can warm them up and serve them with fresh, unsweetened whipped cream for a quick dessert.

Let's Eat!

PINEAPPLE MOSTARDA

SAN ANDREAS, BELLWETHER FARMS, CALIFORNIA :: RAW SHEEP'S MILK

San Andreas, named after the famed fault line that runs through California, is a great way to shake things up on your cheese plate. This pecorino-style tomme will make you fall in love with sheep's-milk cheeses, if you haven't already. The pineapple mostarda is a little hot and a little sweet, balancing the slightly nutty, gamy notes of the cheese.

YIELD: 2 CUPS
PREP TIME: 10 MINUTES
COOK TIME: 1 HOUR PLUS 30 MINUTES
TOTAL TIME: 4 DAYS

1 ripe pineapple, about 1 pound

8 ounces granulated sugar

⅓ cup orange juice

½ cup dry white wine (e.g., pinot grigio)

1 tablespoon dry mustard powder

Chef's note: Make ahead. It will keep for up to 1 month.

Other cheeses to serve with this accompaniment: Frère fumant, Gruyère, or Roquefort.

Creative suggestion: Combine this mostarda with cilantro, sautéed bell peppers, garlic, and ginger to create a sweet, spicy sauce. Add some chicken and serve over rice.

Trim the top and outer layer from the pineapple. Cut off the four sides lengthwise from around the core. Discard the core. Slice the flesh into 1-inch pieces.

In a medium mixing bowl, toss together the pineapple, sugar, and orange juice. Transfer to a heat-proof container, and let sit in the refrigerator for at least 12 hours or overnight.

The next day, strain the liquid and as much sugar as possible into a small saucepan. Return the fruit to the container. Over medium-low heat, bring the strained liquid to a boil. Boil until reduced by half, about 20 minutes. Pour the syrup over the fruit, and refrigerate for at least 12 hours or overnight.

On day two, repeat the straining and cooking process. Pour the syrup over the fruit, and refrigerate for at least 12 hours or overnight.

On the third day, repeat the straining and cooking process.

Transfer the fruit and syrup to a blender. Add the white wine and mustard powder. Blend until smooth, about 2 minutes. Transfer to an airtight container and let cool.

Once cool, place in the refrigerator and keep for 1 day before serving to properly infuse the flavors. Keep refrigerated. Serve at room temperature.

BROCCOLI ANCHOVY PURÉE

TALEGGIO GUSTO ANTICO, ITALY :: RAW COW'S MILK

Don't let the anchovies scare you! For that matter, don't let the broccoli scare you. Taleggio is an Italian classic, washed in brine and aged to have a funk, but not overwhelmingly so. Stinky cheeses are strange beasts. They can often be calmed by pickles, tangy compotes, or mustards. We find that this purée does the trick, too, bringing with it a savory deliciousness. It's all about balance.

YIELD: 2 CUPS
PREP TIME: 10 MINUTES
COOK TIME: 20 MINUTES

3 large stalks broccoli

1 small yellow onion, peeled

7 fillets marinated white anchovies (also known as *boquerones*)

1 tablespoon oil from anchovy marinade

1 tablespoon unsalted butter

1½ teaspoons salt

Cut the florets off the broccoli and break them apart into 1-inch pieces. Set aside. Cut off and discard the bottom inch of each stalk. Peel the tough outer skin off the stalks with a vegetable peeler. Discard the trimmings. Cut the stalks into ¼-inch pieces.

Chop the onion into ¼-inch pieces.

Combine the broccoli florets and stalk, ⅓ cup of water, and the rest of the ingredients in a medium saucepan. Cook over medium heat, covered, for about 10 to 12 minutes, or until soft.

Once the broccoli is soft, transfer the mixture to a blender. Blend on high until smooth.

Scrape the purée into an airtight container and chill. Serve chilled or at room temperature.

Chef's note: Make ahead. It will keep for up to 1 week.

Other cheeses to serve with this accompaniment: Muenster or another strong, savory washed-rind cheese.

Creative suggestion: Mix with mashed potatoes and bake for a unique version of brandade.

Let's Eat!

SWEET PICKLED CONCORD GRAPES

LA PERAL, SPAIN :: PASTEURIZED COW'S MILK

Concord grapes come for a short time here on the East Coast, always with cooler weather and winter close on their tail. This is an adult combination that will bring up nostalgic memories of sweet, sticky PB&J sammies.

YIELD: 4 CUPS
PREP TIME: 10 MINUTES
COOK TIME: 10 MINUTES

1½ pounds seedless Concord grapes (about 3 cups)

1 sprig fresh rosemary, leaves removed from stem and stem discarded

½ cup champagne vinegar

½ cup rice vinegar

1 cup granulated sugar

½ teaspoon black pepper

Pinch of salt

Remove the stems from the grapes. Pierce the stem end of each grape with the tip of a paring knife, creating a small *X*. Place the grapes and rosemary in a glass pickling jar.

In a medium saucepan, combine 1 cup of water and the remaining ingredients. Bring to a boil, stirring occasionally. Remove from the heat and let cool for 10 minutes.

Pour the pickling liquid over the grapes until it covers the grapes completely. Immediately place the lid on the jar while the mixture is still warm.

Refrigerate for 2 days before serving to properly infuse the flavors.

Chef's notes: We are fortunate to have seedless Concords from upstate New York available at the green market. They are a smaller variety but still packed with high flavor. If seedless Concord grapes are unavailable in your area, you can cut them in half and remove the seeds by hand, but this is a tedious project. You can also substitute red or black seedless grapes.

Make ahead. They will keep for 2 weeks.

Other cheeses to serve with this accompaniment: Chevrolait or another sweet, intense blue.

Creative suggestion: Toss these with arugula, toasted nuts, and crumbled blue cheese. Drizzle with a little olive oil and pickling juice for your vinaigrette.

Let's Eat!

A cheese might look like this as a whole wheel.

A cheese might look like this as a whole wheel.

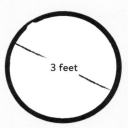

3 feet

The cheesemonger cuts off a piece like this for you to take home

The cheesemonger cuts a piece like this for you to take home

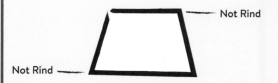

Not Rind

Not Rind

You cut it up like this for your event. First like a pie:

You cut it up like this for your event, into large matchstick shaped portions:

Then each pie piece into thin, one ounce, single servings:

Rind

Center of wheel

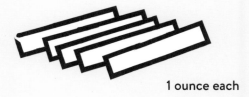

1 ounce each

A log like Boucheron can just be sliced:

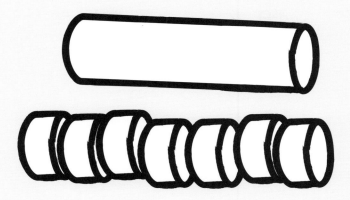

Cut small, round cheeses like a pie.

Even if they are square:

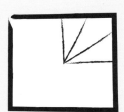

Don't cut off your cheese slice's nose:

Or cut an edge off:

Little cheeses can be cut like pies, too:

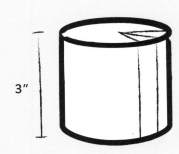

3"

These guides are intended to be accessible tools to help you make a quick pairing decision from the many condiments and cheeses featured in this book. If you are starting with a particular accompaniment, find it in the column on the left of the condiment pairing chart and see suggested cheese pairings to the right. If you are starting with a particular cheese, find it on the left of the cheese pairing chart and see suggested accompaniments to the right. Please do not limit yourself to only these suggestions; the combinations are endless!

CHEESE PAIRING GUIDE

CHEESE	CONDIMENT A
3-Corner Field Farm Frère Fumant	Sweet and Sour Pineapple
Alemar Cheese Company Good Thunder	Chipotle Cumin Mustard
Alta Langa La Tur	Stewed Strawberries
Arpea de Brebis	Coffee Cajeta
Baetje Farms Bloomsdale	Rosé Rhubarb
Barbablu	Pink-Pepper Pickled Rhubarb
Beehive Cheese Company Barely Buzzed	Anise Meringue
Bellwether Farms San Andreas	Pineapple Mostarda
Bleu des Basques	Smoky Pickled Okra
Boxcarr Cottonseed	Parsnip Purée
Brillat-Savarin	Spring Pea and Sweet Onion Purée
Calkins Creamery Georgic	Brandy Poached Pears
Caña de Cabra	Lovely Lemon Saffron Marshmallows
Capriole Goat Cheese O'Banon	Bourbon Walnuts
Capriole Goat Cheese Wabash Cannonball	Fava Bean Pesto
Cato Corner Farm Hooligan	Spiced Pear Cider Reduction
Chällerhocker	Roasted Cipollini Onions
Colston Bassett Stilton	Savory Cherry Chutney
Consider Bardwell Pawlet	Bacon Molasses Mustard
Cowgirl Creamery Red Hawk	Blood Orange Fennel Chip
Crémeux des Augustins	Mushroom Duxelles
Cypress Grove Humboldt Fog	Blackberry Honey

CONDIMENT B	CONDIMENT C
Savory Cherry Chutney	Smoky Honey Mustard
Roasted Cipollini Onions	Smoky Pickled Okra
Passionfruit Basil-Seed Curd	Salted Chocolate Graham Cracker
Orange Confit	Sweet and Spicy Apple Chutney
Sweet and Spicy Red Pepper Jelly	Rosemary Rhubarb Jelly
Anise Meringue	Green Tea White Chocolate Fudge
Rosemary Pine Nuts	Orange Confit
Blood Orange Fennel Chip	Sweet and Sour Pineapple
Dilly Carrots	Lemon Roasted Asparagus
Fava Bean Pesto	Mushroom Duxelles
Herbes de Provence Caramel Corn	Spiced Carrot Chutney
Rosé Rhubarb	Stewed Strawberries
Sweet and Spicy Red Pepper Jelly	Spring Pea and Sweet Onion Purée
Brandy Poached Pears	Summer Peach Compote
Spring Pea and Sweet Onion Purée	Sweet and Spicy Red Pepper Jelly
Smoky Honey Mustard	Orange Confit
Smoky Pickled Okra	Herb-Butter Poached Potatoes
Red Wine Shallots	Brandy Poached Pears
Spicy Curry Cashew Brittle	Fried Pepitas
Carrot Cumin Purée	Parsnip Purée
Lush Leeks	Fried Pepitas
Fava Bean Pesto	Rosemary Rhubarb Jelly

Cheese Pairing Guide

CHEESE	CONDIMENT A
Di Stefano Burrata alla Panna	Summer Peach Compote
El Cortijo Manchego Añejo	Dilly Carrots
Époisses	Shiitake Salad
Goat Lady Dairy Providence	Rosemary Pine Nuts
Gorgonzola Dolce	Sweet Balsamic Pickled Figs
Gourmino Gruyère 18 Month	Castelvetrano Olive Lemon Tapenade
Green Dirt Farm Fresh	Kale Pesto
Grevenbroeker	Green Tea White Chocolate Fudge
Ibores	Sweet and Sour Lotus Root
Jacobs & Brichford Ameribella	Red Wine Shallots
Jacquin Carré du Berry	Rosemary Rhubarb Jelly
Jacquin Chèvre	Passionfruit Basil-Seed Curd
Jasper Hill Farm Bayley Hazen	Salted Chocolate Graham Cracker
Jasper Hill Farm Winnimere	Maple Roasted Apples
Käserei Zurwies Ziege Rot	Lush Leeks
La Peral	Sweet Pickled Concord Grapes
Lazy Lady Farm Thin Red Line	Sweet and Spicy Red Pepper Jelly
Lively Run Goat Dairy Cayuga Blue	Honeycomb
Marcelli Formaggi Ricotta Scorza Nera	Sun-Dried Tomato Pesto
Mimolette	Smoky Honey Mustard
Narragansett Creamery Renaissance Ricotta	Husk Cherry Jam
Nettle Meadow Farm Kunik	Deviled-Egg Cream
Old Chatham Ewe's Blue	Kiwi Mostarda
Ossau-Iraty	Brown Sugar Fudge
Parish Hill Herdsman	Spicy Curry Cashew Brittle
Pecorino Foglie	Laced Balsamic Reduction
Premium Marieke Gouda	Orange Confit
Prodigal Farm Chevrolait	Tomato Caraway Chutney
Quattro Portoni Casatica di Bufala	Coconut Macaroons
Quattro Portoni Surfin' Blu	Balsamic Rosemary Cherry Mustard
Quicke's Vintage Cheddar	Bacon Love
River's Edge Chèvre Up in Smoke	Buttered Pecans

CONDIMENT B	CONDIMENT C
Kale Pesto	Tomato Confit
Chipotle Cumin Mustard	Smoky Pickled Okra
Red Wine Shallots	Fried Pepitas
Sun-Dried Tomato Pesto	Herbes de Provence Caramel Corn
Blackberry Honey	Bacon Love
Fried Pepitas	Smoky Honey Mustard
Lovely Lemon Saffron Marshmallows	Coconut Pineapple Cajeta
Kiwi Mostarda	Cardamom Poached Butternut Squash
Sun-Dried Tomato Pesto	Dilly Carrots
Bacon Molasses Mustard	Lush Leeks
Coconut Macaroons	Blackberry Honey
Baba Ghanoush	Spring Pea and Sweet Onion Purée
Rosemary Pine Nuts	Bacon Love
Savory Cherry Chutney	Bourbon Walnuts
Spring Pea and Sweet Onion Purée	Fava Bean Pesto
Dilly Carrots	Brown Sugar Fudge
Fava Bean Pesto	Spring Pea and Sweet Onion Purée
Sweet Pickled Concord Grapes	Kale Pesto
Laced Balsamic Reduction	Pineapple Mostarda
Sweet and Sour Lotus Root	Smoky Pickled Okra
Kale Pesto	Summer Peach Compote
Creamed Corn	Husk Cherry Jam
Herbes de Provence Caramel Corn	Green Tea White Chocolate Fudge
Anise Meringue	Buttered Pecans
Herb-Butter Poached Potatoes	Smoky Honey Mustard
Sun-Dried Tomato Pesto	Tomato Caraway Chutney
Spicy Curry Cashew Brittle	Buttered Pecans
Smoky Pickled Okra	Shiitake Salad
Blood Orange Fennel Chip	Coffee Cajeta
Tomato Confit	Sweet Balsamic Pickled Figs
Smoky Honey Mustard	Rosemary Pine Nuts
Salted Chocolate Graham Cracker	Brandy Poached Pears

Cheese Pairing Guide

CHEESE	CONDIMENT A
Roelli Cheese Haus Dunbarton Blue	Sweet and Spicy Apple Chutney
Rogue River Blue	Toasted Walnut Pesto
Rollingstone Chèvre	Baba Ghanoush
Roquefort	Herbes de Provence Caramel Corn
Rosso di Langa	Cardamom Poached Butternut Squash
Sequatchie Cove Dancing Fern	Golden Cauliflower Purée
Sierra Nevada Gina Marie Cream Cheese	Coconut Pineapple Cajeta
Spoonwood Cabin Feta	Carrot Cumin Purée
Sweet Grass Dairy Green Hill	Creamed Corn
Taleggio Gusto Antico	Broccoli Anchovy Purée
Mozzarella Company Mozzarella	Tomato Confit
Tomme Brulée	Fried Pepitas
Uplands Cheese Pleasant Ridge Reserve	Herb-Butter Poached Potatoes
Vermont Creamery Coupole	Spicy Carrot Chutney
Von Trapp Farmstead Mad River Blue	Roasted Asparagus
Vulto Creamery Ouleout	Pickled Fennel

CONDIMENT PAIRING GUIDE

CONDIMENT	CHEESE A
Anise Meringue	Beehive Cheese Company Barely Buzzed
Apple Chutney	Roelli Cheese Haus Dunbarton Blue
Baba Ghanoush	Rollingstone Chèvre
Bacon Love	Quicke's Vintage Cheddar
Bacon Molasses Mustard	Consider Bardwell Pawlet
Balsamic Rosemary Cherry Mustard	Quattro Portoni Surfin' Blu
Blackberry Honey	Cypress Grove Humboldt Fog
Bourbon Walnuts	Capriole Goat Cheese O'Banon
Brandy Poached Pears	Calkins Creamery Georgic
Broccoli Anchovy Purée	Taleggio Gusto Antico
Brown Sugar Fudge	Ossau-Iraty

CONDIMENT B	CONDIMENT C
Honeycomb	Herbes de Provence Caramel Corn
Brandy Poached Pears	Spiced Pear Cider Reduction
Tomato Confit	Kale Pesto
Husk Cherry Jam	Sweet and Sour Pineapple
Rosemary Pine Nuts	Coconut Macaroons
Deviled-Egg Cream	Toasted Walnut Pesto
Sweet and Spicy Apple Chutney	Stewed Strawberries
Castelvetrano Olive Lemon Tapenade	Spiced Carrot Chutney
Shiitake Salad	Deviled-Egg Cream
Cardamom Poached Butternut Squash	Red Wine Shallots
Kale Pesto	Castelvetrano Olive Lemon Tapenade
Toasted Walnut Pesto	Rosemary Pine Nuts
Spicy Curry Cashew Brittle	Bourbon Walnuts
Fava Bean Pesto	Rosemary Rhubarb Jelly
Herbes de Provence Caramel Corn	Savory Cherry Chutney
Chipotle Cumin Mustard	Shiitake Salad

CHEESE B	CHEESE C
Barbablu	American Cheddar
Jeffs' Select Gouda	Fontina Val d'Aosta
Arethusa Dairy Farmer's Cheese	Fresh cheeses
French Muenster	Alpine-style cheeses
Twin Maple Farm Hudson Red	French Muenster
Stilton	Strong blues
Lazy Lady Trillium	Mild blues or aged goat cheeses
Goat Lady Dairy Providence	Firm nutty cheeses and Cheddar
Rogue Creamery Oregon Blue	Fresh cheeses or mild blues
Cricket Creek Farm Tobasi	Meaty, washed-rind cheeses
Landmark Creamery Anabasque	Firm, nutty cheeses and strong blues

Condiment Pairing Guide

CONDIMENT	CHEESE A
Buttered Pecans	River's Edge Chèvre Up in Smoke
Cardamom Poached Butternut Squash	Rosso di Langa
Carrot Cumin Purée	Spoonwood Cabin Feta
Castelvetrano Olive Lemon Tapenade	Gourmino Gruyère 18 Month
Chipotle Cumin Mustard	Alemar Cheese Company Good Thunder
Chocolate Graham Cracker	Jasper Hill Farm Bayley Hazen
Coconut Pineapple Cajeta	Sierra Nevada Gina Marie Cream Cheese
Coconut Macaroons	Quattro Portoni Casatica di Bufala
Coffee Cajeta	Arpea de Brebis
Creamed Corn	Sweet Grass Dairy Green Hill
Deviled-Egg Cream	Nettle Meadow Farm Kunik
Dilly Carrots	El Cortijo Manchego Añejo
Fava Bean Pesto	Capriole Goat Cheese Wabash Cannonball
Fried Pepitas	Tomme Brulée
Golden Cauliflower Purée	Sequatchie Cove Dancing Fern
Green Tea White Chocolate Fudge	Grevenbroeker
Herb-Butter Poached Potatoes	Uplands Cheese Pleasant Ridge Reserve
Herbes de Provence Caramel Corn	Roquefort
Honeycomb	Lively Run Goat Dairy Cayuga Blue
Husk Cherry Jam	Narragansett Creamery Renaissance Ricotta
Kale Pesto	Green Dirt Farm Fresh
Kiwi Mostarda	Old Chatham Ewe's Blue
Laced Balsamic Reduction	Marcelli Formaggi Ricotta Scorza Nera
Lemon Roasted Asparagus	Von Trapp Farmstead Mad River Blue
Lovely Lemon Saffron Marshmallows	Caña de Cabra
Lush Leeks	Käserei Zurwies Anton's Ziege Rot
Maple Roasted Apples	Jasper Hill Farm Winnimere
Mushroom Duxelles	Crémeux des Augustins
Orange Confit	Premium Marieke Gouda 18 Months
Blood Orange Fennel Chip	Cowgirl Creamery Red Hawk
Parsnip Purée	Boxcarr Cottonseed
Passionfruit Basil-Seed Curd	Jacquin Chèvre

CHEESE B	CHEESE C
Capriole Goat Cheese O'Banon	Firm, nutty cheeses and Cheddar
Mystic Cheese Company Melville	Bloomy and mild washed cheeses
Ibores	Fresh cheeses or firm goat's-milk cheeses
Bellwether Farms San Andreas	Firm, nutty cheeses
Sbrinz	Washed rind and Alpine-style cheeses
Salvatore Bklyn Smoked Ricotta	Fresh, bloomy, and mild blue cheeses
Petit Billy	Fresh cheeses
Robiola Bosina	Fresh, bloomy, and mild washed cheeses
Woodcock Farm Timberdoodle	Washed-rind cheeses
Boxcarr Cottonbell	Bloomy-rind cheeses
Sequatchie Cove Dancing Fern	Bloomy-rind cheeses
Cato Corner Farm Womanchego	Manchego or firm, nutty cheeses
Old Chatham Camembert Square	Fresh and bloomy cheeses
Ovelha Amanteigado	Firm, nutty cheeses
Spoonwood Cabin Cabinbert	Bloomy and washed-rind cheeses
Blue Ledge Farm Middlebury Blue	Mild blues
Spring Brook Farm Reading Raclette	Alpine style cheeses
Abondance	Mild bloomy cheeses and strong blues
Pleasant Ridge Reserve	Alpine style cheeses, Cheddar, and strong blues
Baetje Bloomsdale	Mascarpone and fresh cheeses
Il Vegetale	Fresh, bloomy, and firm cheeses
King Island Dairy Roaring Forties Blue	Strong, fruity blue cheeses
Piave Vecchio	Parmigiano-Reggiano and firm sharp cheeses
Plymouth Artisan Cheese Big Blue	Strong Alpine style cheeses
Casatica di Bufala	Fresh, and bloomy cheeses
Grès des Vosges	Bloomy and washed-rind cheeses
Uplands Cheese Rush Creek Reserve	Mild washed rind cheeses
Alemar Cheese Company Bent River	Brie or savory bloomy rind cheeses
Grafton Village Bear Hill	Cheddar and firm sheep's-milk cheeses
Bleating Heart Fat Bottom Girl	Cheddar and firm sheep's-milk cheeses
Von Trapp Farmstead Mt. Alice	Brie or savory bloomy rind cheeses
Selles-sur-Cher	Mascarpone and fresh cheeses

Condiment Pairing Guide

CONDIMENT	CHEESE A
Pickled Fennel	Vulto Creamery Ouleout
Pickled Rhubarb	Barbablu
Pineapple Mostarda	Bellwether Farms San Andreas
Red Wine Shallots	Jacobs & Brichford Ameribella
Roasted Cipollini Onions	Chällerhocker
Rosé Rhubarb	Baetje Farms Bloomsdale
Rosemary Pine Nuts	Goat Lady Dairy Providence
Rosemary Rhubarb Jelly	Jacquin Carré du Berry
Savory Cherry Chutney	Colston Bassett Stilton
Shiitake Salad	Époisses
Smoky Honey Mustard	Mimolette
Smoky Pickled Okra	Bleu des Basques
Spiced Carrot Chutney	Vermont Creamery Coupole
Spiced Pear Cider Reduction	Cato Corner Farm Hooligan
Spicy Curry Cashew Brittle	Parish Hill Herdsman
Spring Pea and Sweet Onion Purée	Brillat-Savarin
Stewed Strawberries	Alta Langa La Tur
Summer Peach Compote	Di Stefano Burrata alla Panna
Sun-Dried Tomato Pesto	Pecorino Foglie
Sweet and Sour Lotus Root	Ibores
Sweet and Sour Pineapple	3-Corner Field Farm Frère Fumant
Sweet and Spicy Red Pepper Jelly	Lazy Lady Farm Thin Red Line
Sweet Balsamic Pickled Figs	Gorgonzola Dolce
Sweet Pickled Concord Grapes	La Peral
Toasted Walnut Pesto	Rogue River Blue
Tomato Confit	Mozzarella Company Mozzarella
Tomato Caraway Chutney	Prodigal Farm Chevrolait

CHEESE B	CHEESE C
Jasper Hill Willoughby	Strong washed rind cheeses
Tomme Chèvre	Fresh and firm sheep's- or goat's-milk cheeses
Ewephoria	Pecorino or firm sheep's-milk cheese
Wisconsin Sheep Co-op Blue Hills Bleu	Taleggio or strong washed rind cheeses
Alemar Cheese Company Good Thunder	Alpine style or savory washed rind cheeses
Many Fold Farm Condor's Ruin	Fresh and bloomy cheeses
Bonnieview Farms Ben Nevis	Firm, nutty cheeses
Fleur du Maquis	Fresh and bloomy cheeses
Stinking Bishop	Washed rinds and strong blues
Von Trapp Oma	Washed rinds and firm, earthy cheeses
Stompetoren Grand Cru	Alpine-style cheeses
Roquefort	Strong blue cheeses
Briar Rose Creamery Freya's Wheel	Bloomy and washed rind cheeses
Ram Hall Dairy Berkswell	Washed rind and mild blues
Fiscalini San Joaquin Gold	Alpine-style and firm cheeses
Cowgirl Creamery Mt. Tam	Brie, fresh and bloomy cheeses
Délice de Bourgogne	Fresh and bloomy cheeses
Doe Run Farm Hummingbird	Fresh and bloomy cheeses
Parmigiano-Reggiano	Firm, sharp cheeses
Fontal	Firm goat's- or sheep's-milk cheeses
Idiazabal	Alpine style cheeses
Cypress Grove Humboldt Fog	Bloomy goat's-milk cheeses
Verde Capra	Firm sheep's-milk cheeses
Danish Blue	Strong blue cheeses
Reblochon	Bloomy, washed-rind, and mild blue cheeses
Quadrello di Bufala	Fresh, bloomy, and washed-rind cheeses
Stracapra	Alpine style, washed rind and strong blues

Condiment Pairing Guide

INDEX

Note: Page references in *italics* indicate photographs.

A

Accompaniments
  about the recipes, 14–15
  buying ingredients for, 86, 109
  favorite contrasts, 87–88
  fresh local produce for, 109
  leftover, uses for, 14–15, 86
  pairing with cheeses, 19, 86–88
  presenting, on serving platter, 170–171
  store-bought options for, 10, 14
Affinage, 78–79
Airtight containers, 16
Ameribella (Jacobs & Brichford Farmstead Cheese), 77, *82*, 83
Anchovy Broccoli Purée, *192*, 199
Anise Meringue, *139*, *148*, 148–149
Anton's Ziege Rot (Käserei Zurwies), *192*, 195
Apple(s)
  Chutney, Sweet and Spicy, *181*, 191
  Maple Roasted, 67, 72, *73*
Arpea de Brebis (France), 55, 62
Asparagus, Lemon Roasted, *127*, 136, *137*

B

Baba Ghanoush, *116*, 120–121
Bacon Love, *181*, 186, *187*
Bacon Molasses Mustard, *126*, 134–135
Balsamic Pickled Figs, Sweet, *156*, 167
Balsamic Reduction, Laced, 67, 76
Balsamic Rosemary Cherry Mustard, 55, 63
Barbablu (Italy), *108*, 114
Barely Buzzed (Beehive Cheese Company), *139*, 148
Basil-Seed Passionfruit Curd, 45, *48*, 48–49
Bayley Hazen Blue (Jasper Hill Farm), *152*, 154
Bean, Fava, Pesto, *156*, 160, *161*
Beverages, pairing with cheese, 140–143
Blackberry Honey, 77, 80
Blood Orange Fennel Chip, *139*, 146, *147*
Bloomsdale (Baetje Farms), *108*, 112
Bourbon Walnuts, *84*, 90
Brandy Poached Pears, *192*, 196, 196–197
Bread, serving cheese with, 98–99
Brevibacterium linens (B. linens), 26
Brillat-Savarin (France), *20*, 29
Brittle, Spicy Curry Cashew, *156*, 162–163
Broccoli Anchovy Purée, *192*, 199
Brown Sugar Fudge, 77, 81

Buffalo's milk

    Casatica di Bufala (Quattro Portoni), *45*, 50

    cheeses made from, 47

    Surfin' Blu (Quattro Portoni), 55, 63

Burrata alla Panna (Di Stefano Cheese), 55, 59

Butter, for recipes, 16

Butternut Squash, Cardamom Poached, *84*, 89, *91*

C

Cajeta

    Coconut Pineapple, *156*, 166

    Coffee, 55, 62

Caña de Cabra (Spain), *36*, 40

Caramel Corn, Herbes de Provence, *21*, *34*, 34–35

Caraway Tomato Chutney, *67*, *74*, 74–75

Cardamom Poached Butternut Squash, *84*, 89, *91*

Carré du Berry (Fromagerie Jacquin), *108*, 113

Carrot(s)

    Chutney, Spiced, *127*, *130*, 131

    Cumin Purée, *138*, *144*, 145

    Dilly, *85*, 92

Casatica di Bufala (Quatttro Portoni), *45*, 50

Cashew Brittle, Spicy Curry, *156*, 162–163

Cauliflower Purée, Golden, *169*, 178

Cayuga Blue (Lively Run Goat Dairy), *117*, 124

Chällerhocker (Switzerland), *85*, 93

Cheese

    bloomy and soft, about, 24

    blue, about, 27

    blue, aging process, 69

    buying from cheesemongers, 37

    categories of, 22–27

    cooked and pressed, about, 25

    environmental variations, 128

    farmstead, about, 79

    fresh, about, 23

    how it is made, 68–69

    industrial versus "real," 118

    influenced by seasons, 109–111

    for lactose intolerant, 56

    learning about, 37

    living microflora in, 118–119

    local, buying, 129–130

    Old World styles, 129

    pairing beverages with, 140–143

    for pregnant women, 57, 58

    regional variations, 128–130

    rinds, about, 193

    ripening (affinage), 78–79

    serving at room temperature, 183, 193

    serving with crackers or bread, 98–99

    storing, 182–183

    substituting, note about, 15

    tasting, tips for, 193–194

    uncooked and pressed, about, 25

    washed-rind, about, 26

    washed-rind, aging process, 69

    wrapping, 182–183

Cheesemongers, 37

Cheese plates

   at Casellula, 7–9

   cutting or slicing cheese for, 172

   experimenting with, 9–10

   focus and balance in, 157–159

   for larger parties, 153

   for one person, 153

   order of cheeses on, 170, 171

   pairing cheese with accompaniments, 19, 86–88

   serving platters for, 170

   for sharing at the table, 153

   store-bought options for, 10, 14

Cherry

   Balsamic Rosemary Mustard, 55, 63

   Chutney, Savory, 85, 95

Chèvre (Fromagerie Jacquin), 45, 48

Chèvre (Rollingstone), 116, 120

Chevrolait (Prodigal Farm), 67, 74

Chipotle Cumin Mustard, 36, 42

Chocolate

   Graham Cracker, Salted, 152, 154–155

   White, Green Tea Fudge, 169, 179

Chutney

   Apple, Sweet and Spicy, 181, 191

   Carrot, Spiced, 127, 130, 131

   Cherry, Savory, 85, 95

   Tomato Caraway, 67, 74, 74–75

Coconut

   Macaroons, 45, 50–51

   Pineapple Cajeta, 156, 166

Coffee Cajeta, 55, 62

Compote

   Husk Cherry, 20, 28

   Summer Peach, 55, 59

Concord Grapes, Sweet Pickled, 192, 201

Confit, Tomato, 180, 184–185

Corn, Creamed, 180, 190

Cottonseed (Boxcarr Handmade Cheese), 55, 60

Coupole (Vermont Creamery), 127, 131

Cow's milk. See also specific types below

   cheeses made from, 46

Cow's milk (pasteurized)

   Barely Buzzed, 139, 148

   Brillat-Savarin, 20, 29

   Burrata alla Panna, 55, 59

   Cottonseed, 55, 60

   Crémeaux des Augustins, 138, 150

   Dunbarton Blue, 181, 191

   Époisses, 156, 165

   Fresh Mozzarella, 180, 184

   Georgic, 192, 196

   Gina Marie Cream Cheese, 156, 166

   Good Thunder, 36, 42

   Gorgonzola Dolce, 156, 167

   Green Hill, 180, 190

   Grevenbroeker, 169, 179

   Kunik, 66, 71

   La Peral, 192, 201

   La Tur, 97, 102

   Mimolette (eighteen-month), 96, 103

   Red Hawk, 139, 146

   Renaissance Ricotta, 20, 28

   Rosso di Langa, 84, 89

   Vintage Cheddar, 181, 186, 187

Cow's milk (raw)

Ameribella, *77, 82*, 83

Bayley Hazen Blue, *152*, 154

Dancing Fern, *169*, 178

Feta, *138*, 145

Gruyère Eighteen Month, *169*, 173

Herdsman, *156*, 162

Hooligan, *21*, 32

Mad River Blue, *127*, 136

Ouleout, *97*, 105

Pawlet, *126*, 134

Pleasant Ridge Reserve, *44*, 52

Premium Gouda 18 Month, *181, 188*, 189

Rogue River Blue, *139*, 151

Stilton, *85*, 95

Taleggio Gusto Antico, *192*, 199

Tomme Brulée, *36, 38*, 39

Winnimere, *67*, 72

Cow's milk (thermalized)

Chällerhocker, *85*, 93

Crackers, serving cheese with, 98–99

Crémeaux des Augustins (France), *138*, 150

Cumin

Carrot Purée, *138, 144*, 145

Chipotle Mustard, *36*, 42

Curd, Passionfruit Basil-Seed, *45, 48*, 48–49

Curds and whey, 68–69

Curry Cashew Brittle, Spicy, *156*, 162–163

D

Dairy allergies, 56

Dancing Fern (Sequatchie Cove Creamery), *169*, 178

Deviled-Egg Cream, *66, 70*, 71

Dilly Carrots, *85*, 92

Dunbarton Blue (Roelli Cheese Haus), *181*, 191

E

E. coli, 57–58

Eggplant

Baba Ghanoush, *116*, 120–121

Egg(s)

Deviled-, Cream, *66, 70*, 71

for recipes, 16

Époisses (France), *156*, 165

Equipment and ingredients, 16–17

Ewe's Blue (Old Chatham Sheepherding Company), *96*, 106

F

Fava Bean Pesto, *156, 160, 161*

Fennel

Blood Orange, Chip, *139, 146, 147*

Pickled, *97, 104*, 105

Feta (Spoonwood Cabin), *138*, 145

Figs, Sweet Balsamic Pickled, *156*, 167

Frère Fumant (3-Corner Field Farm), *168*, 176

Fresh (Green Dirt Farm), *168, 174*, 175

Fresh Mozzarella (Mozzarella Company), *180*, 184

Fudge

Brown Sugar, *77*, 81

Green Tea White Chocolate, *169*, 179

G

Georgic (Calkins Creamery), *192*, 196

Geotrichum candidum, 24

Gina Marie Cream Cheese (Sierra Nevada Cheese Co.), *156*, 166

Goat's milk. *See also specific categories below*

    cheeses made from, 47

Goat's milk (pasteurized)

    Anton's Ziege Rot, *192*, 195

    Barbablu, *108*, 114

    Bloomsdale, *108*, 112

    Caña de Cabra, *36*, 40

    Carré du Berry, *108*, 113

    Chèvre (Fromagerie Jacquin), *45*, 48

    Chèvre (Rollingstone), *116*, 120

    Chevrolait, *67*, 74

    Cottonseed, *55*, 60

    Coupole, *127*, 131

    Humbolt Fog, *77*, 80

    Kunik, *66*, 71

    La Tur, *97*, 102

    O'Banon, *84*, 90

    Providence, *55*, 65

    Thin Red Line, *126*, *132*, 133

    Up in Smoke, *96*, 100

    Wabash Cannonball, *156*, 160, *161*

Goat's milk (raw)

    Cayuga Blue, *117*, 124

    Ibores, *116*, 123

Good Thunder (Alemar Cheese Company), *36*, 42

Gorgonzola Dolce (Italy), *156*, 167

Graham Cracker, Salted Chocolate, *152*, 154–155

Green Hill (Sweet Grass Dairy), *180*, 190

Green Tea White Chocolate Fudge, *169*, 179

Grevenbroeker (Belgium), *169*, 179

Gruyère Eighteen Month (Gourmino), *169*, 173

H

Herb-Butter Poached Potatoes, 44, 52, *53*

Herbes de Provence Caramel Corn, *21*, *34*, 34–35

Herdsman (Parish Hill Creamery), *156*, 162

Honey

    Blackberry, *77*, 80

    Honeycomb, *117*, 124, *125*

    Mustard, Smoky, *96*, 103

Hooligan (Cato Corner Farm), *21*, 32

Humbolt Fog (Cypress Grove), *77*, 80

Husk Cherry Compote, *20*, 28

I

Ibores (Spain), *116*, 123

Ice bath, 17

Ingredients and equipment, 16–17

J

Jelly

    Rosemary Rhubarb, *108*, 113

    Sweet and Spicy Red Pepper, *126*, *132*, 133

K

Kale Pesto, *168, 174,* 175
Kiwi Mostarda, *96,* 106, *107*
Kunik (Nettle Meadow Farm), 66, 71

L

Lactose intolerance, 56
La Peral (Spain), *192,* 201
La Tur (Alta Langa), *97,* 102
Leeks, Lush, *192,* 195
Lemon
    Roasted Asparagus, *127,* 136, *137*
    Saffron Marshmallows, Lovely, *36, 40,*
      40–41
Listeria, 57–58
Lotus Root, Sweet and Sour, *116, 122,* 123

M

Macaroons, Coconut, *45,* 50–51
Mad River Blue (Von Trapp Farmstead), *127,*
    136
Manchego Añejo (El Cortijo), *85,* 92
Maple Roasted Apples, *67, 72, 73*
Marshmallows, Lovely Lemon Saffron, *36, 40,*
    40–41
Measuring cups, 17
Meringue, Anise, *139, 148,* 148–149
Micro zester (rasp grater), 17
Milk allergies, 56
Mimolette (eighteen-month) (France), *96,*
    103
Mitibleu (Spain), *44,* 54
Mold spores, 24, 27, 69, 128

Mostarda
    Kiwi, *96,* 106, *107*
    Pineapple, *192,* 198
Mushroom(s)
    Duxelles, *138,* 150
    Shiitake Salad, *156, 164,* 165
Mustard
    Bacon Molasses, *126,* 134–135
    Balsamic Rosemary Cherry, *55,* 63
    Chipotle Cumin, *36,* 42
    Smoky Honey, *96,* 103

O

O'Banon (Capriole Goat Cheese), *84,* 90
Okra, Smoky Pickled, *44,* 54
Olive, Castelvetrano, Lemon Tapenade, *169,*
    173
Onion(s)
    Roasted Cipollini, *85, 93, 94*
    Sweet, and Spring Pea Purée, *20,* 29
Orange
    Blood, Fennel Chip, *139, 146, 147*
    Confit, *181, 188,* 189
Ossau-Iraty (France), *77,* 81
Ouleout (Vulto Creamery), *97,* 105

P

Parchment paper, 17
Parsnip Purée, *55,* 60, *61*
Passionfruit Basil-Seed Curd, *45, 48,* 48–49
Pasteurization, 57, 69
Pawlet (Consider Bardwell Farm), *126,* 134
Pea, Spring, and Sweet Onion Purée, *20,* 29

Peach Compote, Summer, *55*, 59

Pear Cider Reduction, Spiced, *21*, 32–33

Pears, Brandy Poached, *192*, *196*, 196–197

Pecans, Buttered, *96*, 100, *101*

Pecorino Foglie (Italy), *20*, 31

Penicillium candidum, 24, 27

Pepitas, Fried, *36*, *38*, 39

Pepper, Red, Jelly, Sweet and Spicy, *126*, *132*, 133

Pesto

    Fava Bean, *156*, 160, *161*

    Kale, *168*, *174*, 175

    Sun-Dried Tomato, *20*, *30*, 31

    Toasted Walnut, *139*, 151

Pickled Concord Grapes, Sweet, *192*, 201

Pickled Fennel, *97*, *104*, 105

Pickled Figs, Sweet Balsamic, *156*, 167

Pickled Okra, Smoky, *44*, 54

Pickled Rhubarb, Pink-Pepper, *108*, *114*, *115*

Pineapple

    Coconut Cajeta, *156*, 166

    Mostarda, *192*, 198

    Sweet and Sour, *168*, 176–177, *177*

Pine Nuts, Rosemary, *55*, *64*, 65

Pink-Pepper Pickled Rhubarb, *108*, 114, *115*

Pleasant Ridge Reserve (Uplands Cheese), *44*, 52

Popcorn

    Herbes de Provence Caramel Corn, *21*, *34*, 34–35

Potatoes, Herb-Butter Poached, *44*, 52, 53

Premium Gouda 18 Month (Marieke Gouda), *181*, *188*, 189

Providence (Goat Lady Dairy), *55*, 65

Purée

Carrot Cumin, *138*, *144*, 145

Golden Cauliflower, *169*, 178

Parsnip, *55*, 60, *61*

Spring Pea and Sweet Onion, *20*, 29

R

Rasp grater (micro zester), 17

Red Hawk (Cowgirl Creamery), *139*, 146

Reductions

    Laced Balsamic, *67*, 76

    Spiced Pear Cider, *21*, 32–33

Renaissance Ricotta (Narragansett Creamery), *20*, 28

Rhubarb

    Pink-Pepper Pickled, *108*, *114*, *115*

    Rosé, *108*, 112

    Rosemary Jelly, *108*, 113

Ricotta Scorza Nera (Marcelli Formaggi), *67*, 76

Rogue River Blue (Rogue Creamery), *139*, 151

Roquefort (France), *21*, 34

Rosemary

    Balsamic Cherry Mustard, *55*, 63

    Pine Nuts, *55*, *64*, 65

    Rhubarb Jelly, *108*, 113

Rosé Rhubarb, *108*, 112

Rosso di Langa (Alta Langa), *84*, 89

S

Saffron Lemon Marshmallows, Lovely, *36*, *40*, 40–41

Salad, Shiitake, *156*, *164*, 165

Salt, 17

San Andreas (Bellwether Farms), *192*, 198

Saucepans, 17

Shallots, Red Wine, *77*, *82*, 83

Sheep's milk. *See also specific categories below*
  cheeses made from, 46–47

Sheep's milk (pasteurized)
  Arpea de Brebis, 55, 62
  Ewe's Blue, *96*, 106
  Fresh, *168*, *174*, 175
  La Tur, *97*, 102
  Ossau-Iraty, *77*, 81
  Roquefort, *21*, 34
  Rosso di Langa, *84*, 89

Sheep's milk (raw)
  Frère Fumant, *168*, 176
  Manchego Añejo, *85*, 92
  Mitibleu, *44*, 54
  Pecorino Foglie (Italy), *20*, 31
  Ricotta Scorza Nera, *67*, 76
  San Andreas, *192*, 198

Shiitake Salad, *156*, *164*, 165

Silica gel, 17

Squash, Butternut, Cardamom Poached, *84*, 89, *91*

Stilton (Colston Bassett), *85*, 95

Strawberries, Stewed, *97*, 102

Surfin' Blu (Quattro Portoni), 55, 63

T

Taleggio Gusto Antico (Italy), *192*, 199

Tapenade, Castelvetrano Olive Lemon, *169*, 173

Thermalization, 69

Thin Red Line (Lazy Lady Farm), *126*, *132*, 133

Tomato
  Caraway Chutney, *67*, *74*, 74–75
  Confit, *180*, 184–185
  Sun-Dried, Pesto, *20*, *30*, 31

Tomme Brulée (France), *36*, *38*, 39

U

Up in Smoke (River's Edge), *96*, 100

V

Vanilla beans and extract, 17

Vintage Cheddar (Quicke's), *181*, 186, *187*

W

Wabash Cannonball (Capriole Goat Cheese), *156*, 160, *161*

Walnut(s)
  Bourbon, *84*, 90
  Toasted, Pesto, *139*, 151

Whey, separating from curds, 68

White Chocolate Green Tea Fudge, *169*, 179

Wine
  pairing with cheese, 141–142
  Red, Shallots, *77*, *82*, 83
  Rosé Rhubarb, *108*, 112

Winnimere (Jasper Hill Farm), *67*, 72